AT RISK OF GREATNESS

AT RISK OF GREATNESS

REIMAGINING YOUTH OUTCOMES
THROUGH THE INTERSECTION
OF ART AND TECHNOLOGY

CARLOS CARPIZO

NEW DEGREE PRESS

AT RISK OF GREATNESS

Reimagining Youth Outcomes Through the Intersection of Art and Technology

ISBN   978-1-63676-521-1   *Paperback*
           978-1-63676-055-1   *Kindle Ebook*
           978-1-63676-056-8   *Ebook*

ACKNOWLEDGEMENTS

Above all to my Lord and Savior Jesus Christ.

To my loving and supporting family: Carmen, Carlos, Adriana, Carlos, Jorge, Maricarmen, Sofia, Andres, Victor, and Maggie. Also Pookie, Martha, Lola, and Ted.

Special thanks to Jennifer Ebinger, Eric Koester, Weeda Hamdan, Elsa Grossmann, Christy Mossburg, Carol Thompson, Pea Richelle White, Nicolas Gonzalez, Pablo Raphael, Adriana De Urquidi, Bernardo De Urquidi, Luis Daniel Beltran, Sofia Bastidas, Carlos Gonzalez-Jaime, Michael Lagocki, Andres Ruzo, Jennifer Peterson, Kelly Jenson, and Lonnie Laue.

For taking the time to provide me with the interviews so important to this cause, I'd like to thank Bernardo Rosendo, Fred Villanueva, Pavica Sheldon, James M. Honeycutt, Nicolas Gonzalez, David J. Sullivan, Sixto Cancel, Maria Elisa Wolffer, Tyler Durman, Angelica Mosqueda, Ana-Maria Ramos, Arturo Velez, Amy Dunham, D, Esther Benjamin,

Emmanuel Winkler, Weeda Hamdan, Ben Koch, Graciela Rojas, and Debbie Renteria.

Many thanks to Aidee Granados, Alain Espinosa, Alberto Chalbaud, Alberto Flores Madero, Aldo Figueroa, Alejandro Gutierrez Ponce, Ana Margarita Rivero Arias, Ana Sanchez, Andrea Gean, Andres Alvarez-Cordero, Andrew Barker, Angel Lamuño, Angelica Mora, Ann Danner, Armando Hernandez, Barbara Brown, Barrie Hall, Bindu R. Gross, Bobby Vassallo, Boon Kim Tan, Brad Bush, Braulio Andreu, Brent Keefer, Carlos Gonzalez-Jaime, Caroline Hamrit, Catalina Rodriguez Tapia, Chip DeClue, Chris Armstrong, Christian Angulo, Clarita Borja Hinojosa, Cynthia Nwaubani, David Boyett, David Cannon, David Fremaux, Don McKenna, Duane Knecht, Eduardo Moreno, Eduardo Zaldivar, Edwin Solis, Elsa Buendia, Emilio Garcia, Emilio Pimentel, Eric Edstrom, Eric Koester, Ezio Mura, Fernando Avelar, Fernando Quintero, Francisco de la Torre Galindo, Gary Bedard, Gerardo Raphael, Gildardo Zafra, Guillermo Granados, Guillermo Moreno Lacalle, Hector Ortiz, Jacques M Jean, James Barber, James E McClain, Janet Marcum, Javier Lamuno, Jeronimo Valdez, Jo Thompson, John D Wilson, John J Stewart, John Wilkins, Jorge Azpe, Jose 'Pepe' Gomez, Jose Antonio Lamuño, Jose Eduardo del Valle Diharce, Jose Luis Hernandez, Jose Luis Lamuño, Jose Matuk, Jose Roberto Carvajal, Josefina Maus, Joseph R. Chapa, Josh Balmer, Jovelyn Castellanos, Juan Rolon, Karin Larrave, Kenton Kisler, Larry King, Leticia Castellanos, Luis Gonzalez Sada, Maddalena Loggia, Maria Eugenia Andreu, Mariano Garcia Guajardo, Mario Guerendo, Marshall Wenrich, Mats Lundberg, Mauricio Flores Madero, Mauricio Martinez, Miguel Angel Vazquez Reyes, Miguel Garcia-Rechani, Mikael Calais,

Nelson Valderrama, Pedro Yarahuan, Prisma Garcia, Quincy Ragsdale, Ramir Camu, Rene Larrave, Rhonda Kehlbeck, Ricardo Ceniceros, Ricardo Leal, Robert Chapman, Roberto Keoseyan, Roberto Leal, Rocio Lamuño, Rodney J Stewart, Rodolfo Peña,Ron Robbins, Russ Jaskot, Samuel Dillow, Sergio Hueck, Sergio Robledo, Silvia Montes de Oca, Steve Banta, Susana Andreu, Tanis Cornell, Teri Walker, Theresa Boyce, Ulises Aguilar Nahle, Valeria Schmidt, and Weeda and Maan Hamdan.

CONTENTS

———

INTRODUCTION

———

Please close your eyes. What music
or song comes to your mind?

When writing this book, the first line of one
of my favorite songs came to mind: "The Living Years" by Mike and the Mechanics.

It talks about how each generation blames the one before ….

When listening to this song for the first time, I was younger than my two Gen Z sons today. It evokes very different emotions today compared to those I felt back then. Neither the lyrics nor the music of the song has changed. But I have, and technology has as well.

We're fortunate because, thanks to advances in technology, we're able to listen to any music that comes to mind anytime. We can play a song from the library on our smartphones and even search for it on the internet or through a subscription to a music streaming service. Thanks to technology, we can also discover new music by listening to a broadcast, or through the recommendation of a friend's playlist or an algorithm; all second nature for Gen Zs (born between 1997 and 2012).

Advances in technology are also being used in a predatory way to capture our attention. This disproportionately impacts young adults and those considered Gen Z. The advertisement engines that we call social media are a race to capture the attention of users, rewarding us for spending more time on our screens. Tristan Harris, former Design Ethicist at Google and founder of the Center for Humane Technology, has stated in unequivocal terms that he was part of a control room shaping the thoughts and feelings of internet users.[1] He has been featured on *60 Minutes*, TED, and *PBS News,* among other reputable sources of information.

Teenagers are wired to be rebellious and have an oppositional attitude, and since the global counterculture movement of

---

1   TED, "How a Handful of Tech Companies Control Billions of Minds Every Day | Tristan Harris," July 28, 2017, video, 17:00.

the 1960s, there has been a deliberate effort from society and governments to tame that attitude. Are Gen Zs being rolled over by technology as a result? Is it contributing to the increased number of disoriented individuals? The pace of change of technology that I experienced while growing up as a Gen X pales in comparison to what is being experienced in this twenty-first century.

This significant acceleration of advanced technologies has resulted in an even greater number of choices faced by young people today, making it more difficult for them to make decisions. As a young adult reading this book, I encourage you to keep reading because it will help you understand how to clarify and better manage your education and career choices. If you are a parent or teacher of a young adult, it will help you better understand their point of view and what they're experiencing.

On the educational front, in the past decade, there has been a big push for education in Science, Technology, Engineering, and Mathematics (STEM) fields at all levels to meet current and future demands, reduce the college dropout rates, increase college attendance, and increase graduation rates. I once believed that everyone should go to college. However, I now think differently, and I'm completely against the idea that a college education separates "winners" from "losers," as the vast majority of our society still believes on both sides of the US-Mexico border.

Bryan Caplan, an economist and author, states, "As a society, we continue to push ever larger numbers of students into ever higher levels of education. The main effect is not better jobs or greater skill levels, but a credentialist arms race."[2] For millions of young adults, college provides the education they need for the twenty-first century—one that allows them to do a series of non-routine tasks that require social intelligence, complex critical thinking, and creative problem solving, all key success factors when competing with machines.

But for millions more, college isn't necessarily the best option. While the former are off to a great start, even if a college degree doesn't guarantee success in life, the latter need alternative pathways. In Mexico, "Less than a quarter of the young population (ages twenty-five to thirty-four) have obtained higher education qualifications, and within this limited share of graduates, evidence shows that their skills are not used effectively."[3] In the US every year, over 1.2 million students drop out of high school,[4] and 56 percent of college students who start a four-year college curriculum do not graduate in four years and end up dropping out by year six.[5]

I have had firsthand experience with young adults impacted by this dilemma. As a proud Mexican American myself, I wondered how many "disengaged youth"[6] there were in both

---

2   Bryan Caplan, "The World Might Be Better Off Without College for Everyone," *The Atlantic,* January/February 2018.

3   "Higher Education in Mexico: Labour Market Relevance and Outcomes," OECD, accessed October 15, 2020.

4   "11 Facts about High School Dropout Rates," DoSomething, accessed September 10, 2020.

5   "U.S. College Dropout Rate and Dropout Statistics." CollegeAtlas, Updated Jun 29, 2018, accessed September 10, 2020.

6   Multiple terms exist to identify these youth as well: "ninis" in Mexico (ni estudian ni trabajan), "opportunity youth" in the US, "NEETs" globally (not employed in education or training).

the US and Mexico. This is not an easy answer, as it depends on multiple factors, such as the age bracket or the definitions of employment and underemployment. The simple answer is that the number of them is comparable to the entire population of Mexico in the mid-twentieth century when my parents were born. There are far too many.

We tend to look for technology to solve challenges, and I'm convinced that the STEM fields are necessary. I'm an engineer myself and a terrible guitar player. Because I've had a global career in mobile telecommunications since 1993, I've been in proximity to technological developments that go above and beyond what the average person would experience. Along with the telecom industry, I rode the wave of its convergence, with the information technology industry unleashing the information age. Lately, I've focused more on growing my heart as opposed to my mind, searching for wisdom. I've been an executive for two Fortune 100 companies: Ericsson and Xerox, as well as for a mid-market enterprise with a presence in four countries in the Americas. I've been an entrepreneur, as well. An opportunity to invest in an artificial intelligence company in 2017, along with service in nonprofit boards, opened my mind to think about the impact of our faster future on society at large.

I'm an optimist and firmly believe that society will be better off in the long run thanks to advanced technologies. Yet we cannot turn a blind eye to the many challenges that have surfaced. With further advances in automation and artificial intelligence (AI), we risk ending up thinking like machines and competing with them. We cannot afford that. Machines must exist to improve our human condition.

While launching a social venture in 2019, a collaboration with Mr. Bernardo Rosendo, an arts entrepreneur in the mountains of Guerrero, Mexico, clarified a powerful vision for me: Arts are also essential to help us humans avoid thinking like machines and competing with them. Arts are what make us human.

Take music, for example. The story of music is intertwined with the story of humans, and music has as many functions as technology. Machines can create music or other types of art that convey emotion, and they can do it very well. However, unlike technology, music touches our hearts. It stimulates emotions that are innately human and off-limits to machines.

I believe that the first intersection of art and technology must have taken place tens of thousands of years ago, when our ancestors used or created a tool aimed at survival and developed a rudimentary musical instrument. Maybe our Mayan ancestors had time to develop the concept of zero in mathematics because they just had to pick up a conch shell and blow into it to start creating music.

"The intuitive mind is a sacred gift, and the rational mind is a faithful servant. We have created a society that honors the servant and has forgotten the gift."

This book will give you a glimpse at programs and organizations doing a great job at generating education and employment pathways for youth in general, as well as "disengaged youth" in particular. It will also give you a glimpse of programs and organizations that are doing a great job of improving communities through arts and culture—artists who are also entrepreneurs like Mr. Rosendo identifying and developing assets that matter to the people in the communities where they live and work. If you're an entrepreneur, it will give you concrete ideas for intersecting art and technology.

At the intersection of art and technology lies a huge opportunity—opportunity for society at large and particularly for "at-risk" young adults who represent an abundance of untapped talent as enterprises and communities on both sides of the border who experience a shortage of qualified human capital. By enabling these young adults to develop a success mindset, we will be putting them "At Risk of Greatness."

Carlos Carpizo

TL;DR

Too long. Didn't read.

The book isn't organized in a linear fashion nor is it intended for you to necessarily read in order or from beginning to end.

It packs enough valuable lessons and takeaways for you to start with any chapter that interests you the most.

I hope you do the activity at the beginning of each chapter. You will notice that the images aren't professional except two of them. I did them, and I'm terrible at art. If I did it, YOU can too!

One of the two professional images is a sketch of the mural "Sembrando el Futuro" by Nicolás Gonzalez. It was made in 2019 in the dimensions 8.5 x 24.5 inches with graphite on paper. The other one is the Kosmos logo designed by Nicolás Gonzalez.

I hope that you have read the full Introduction by now, and if you don't want to read all chapters in order, or should you be undecided where to go next, this is what I suggest:

If you are a young adult, I suggest you continue with chapter 6, "Success vs. Success Mindset."

If you are a parent or teacher of a young adult, I suggest you continue with chapter 3, "Smartphones, Social Media, and Gen Zs."

If you are an entrepreneur, I suggest you continue with chapter 8, "The Intersection of Art and Technology."

Enjoy it!

1

THE SLINGSHOT EFFECT
OF THE SMARTPHONE

———

Please take a moment to draw something.

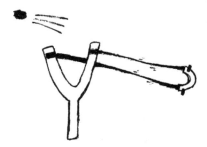

When writing this chapter, I drew this slingshot. I imagine that not many young adults have used one. You hold the frame with one hand and pull back on the elastic material with the other hand, extending it, the pinch-back. When releasing the grip on the elastic material, it contracts, thrusting an object forward.

Our society isn't functioning well in this early part of the twenty-first century. I believe that it is partly due to the unintended consequences of the pace of change of advanced technologies. When the pace exceeds our human ability to adapt to them, they become difficult to manage. As a society, we're experiencing the equivalent effect to the pinch-back of a slingshot.

"In a few hundred years, when the history of our time is written from a long-term perspective, I think it very probable that the most important event those historians will remember is not technology, not the internet, not e-commerce—but the unprecedented change in the human condition."[7]

PETER DRUCKER

Peter Drucker was born in the early twentieth century in Austria. He has been described as the founder of modern management. Many admire Peter Drucker for reasons beyond his positive influence on management in the twentieth century. Among them are his keen eye to observe humanity through individual stories, his wisdom to interpret these stories, and his ability to communicate them. Drucker's

---

7   Bob Buford, *Stuck in Halftime: Reinventing Your One and Only Life* (Grand Rapids, Michigan: Zondervan Publishing House, 2001), Page 9.

primary interest in management was creating conditions for a fully functioning society.

I think of Peter Drucker, the man born before World War I who lived to the beginning of the internet age, and I imagine all the things I wish I could say to him. I imagine myself having a conversation with him before he passed away in 2005.

His first question to me was where I was at the turn of the twenty-first century, when the first millennials were starting to come of age. And I recounted some technology advancements I remembered from that particular point in time:

- Jeff Bezos was featured as *Time* magazine's Person of the Year thanks to Amazon's success in popularizing online shopping.[8]
- Netflix relied on the US Postal Service for delivery of its rental DVDs.[9]
- Google was privately owned and began selling advertisements associated with search keywords.[10]
- In the case of the United States vs. Microsoft, the company was called an "abusive monopoly." [11]
- Sony's PS2 video game console was released as a complete home entertainment console.[12]

---

8 Jeff Bezos, "Person of the Year," *Time,* December 27, 1999.
9 "Netflix's History: From DVD Rentals to Streaming Success," *BBC,* accessed October 15, 2020.
10 "Google's Incredible Growth: A Timeline," *CNN,* accessed October 15, 2020.
11 Joel Brinkley, "U.S. vs. Microsoft: The Overview; U.S. Judge Says Microsoft Violated Antitrust Laws with Predatory Behavior," *The New York Times,* April 4, 2000.
12 *Encyclopedia Britannica Online,* PlayStation2 Electronic Gaming Console.

- Apple announced that it would release its iPod music player; a device that would not only change the way we listen to music but, ultimately, change the entire music industry in less than a decade.[13]

I mentioned that at the turn of the century, I held my first smartphone (Ericsson's R380) with e-mail and limited web browsing capabilities, plus a relatively small grayscale screen that had to be tapped with a plastic stylus that was stored on a slot in the back of the phone.

I described some of the back-then futuristic uses of smartphones since it was still a relatively new concept: conducting a work video conference with multiple participants located in multiple countries while en route to a fun destination with the family. Freedom from being tied to the office and enjoying more time with loved ones. Purchasing movie tickets or gifts from the palm of our hand, from any place and at any time, helping improve relationships.

Smartphones didn't become a reality until Apple launched the iPhone in 2007 as a revolutionary product, paired with AT&T's mobile network for voice and data access, a full two years after Peter's passing. The touch screen's ease of use, combined with the software capabilities built on top of its operating system, indeed made it a product that defined its category.

The software capabilities of smartphones deserve a full chapter. Hardware cannot be overlooked, yet it has become some

---

13 "Apple Presents iPod," Apple Inc., accessed October 15, 2020.

sort of generic building block revolving around microprocessors, wireless connectivity, and input/output sensors. Have you noticed how software has taken over hardware in the pecking order of advances? There are new software languages and programs, or applications from a user interphase standpoint, being created around the clock. We use the software interfacing with a multitude of screens, smart speakers (listening devices), cameras tracking our gestures or movements, or chips implanted in our bodies.

As smartphones became commonplace, we collectively started experiencing what I call the slingshot effect. What do we do in an elevator? Forget about striking a conversation; we hardly say hello or wish a good day to our fellow rider because we're all absorbed in our screens. What do teenagers do when asked to speak to anyone on the phone? They're afraid because they have grown used to communicating via text, chat, or social media. Ninety-five percent of teens own a smartphone or have access to one in the US.[14] And in Mexico, a study found that 75 percent of youth admit to using their smartphone all the time.[15]

Can you picture a group of young adults sitting at a restaurant table taking pictures of themselves, then individually uploading them to their social media accounts as opposed to interacting more with their friends around them? Some unintended consequences of the powerful technology packed into our smartphones represent a setback for our human

14   "Teens, Social Media & Technology 2018," *Pew Research*, accessed October 15, 2020.

15   "El 75% de adolescentes y padres mexicanos, adictos al cellular," *Forbes Mexico*, accessed October 15, 2020.

condition such as less human interaction in the communication form that matches our physical and cognitive evolution over thousands of years. That, I believe, is the pinch-back of the slingshot.

As part of my research, a study titled "Smartphones reduce smiles between strangers"[16] caught my attention. It was performed in 2018, and it shows that smartphones are altering the fabric of social life. In a preregistered experiment, strangers waited together with or without their smartphones; their smiling was later coded by trained assistants. Compared to participants without smartphones, participants with smartphones exhibited significantly fewer smiles of any kind and fewer genuine smiles.

There is no doubt that smartphones, and other smart devices such as tablets, enable mobile collaboration and, when used effectively, like any other tool, improve personal and professional productivity. The examples, such as updating friends and family on good or bad news instantaneously or being able to book a shared vehicle ride, are too many to mention. We benefit from the combined capabilities of processing power, ubiquitous connectivity, increased functionality, and memory storage. Artificial intelligence was rolled out as one of the multiple features since 2011.

The larger question is the impact of smartphones on our human condition in the form of unintended consequences,

16   Kostadin Kushleva, John F. Hunter, Jason Proulx, Sarah D. Pressman, Elizabeth Dunn, "Smartphones Reduce Smiles between Strangers," Elsevier, Computers in Human Behavior, Volume 91, February 2019, Pages 12-16.

such as an increase in feelings of isolation and teenage suicide rates, or business models based on our personal data or attention. Judging from the aforementioned study, and other similar ones, the balance inclines toward the negative. However, I contend that it's too soon to tell.

The good news is that after the pinch-back comes the thrust forward. Ericsson's R380 smartphone was a hybrid mobile phone and personal digital assistant (PDA). Gen Zs don't know that a well-known company marketed a device called Palm Pilot as a PDA when it was a far cry from it. Compared to any smartphone, it would look dumb.

Judith Donath, author of *The Social Machine: Designs for Living Online* and fellow faculty at Harvard University's Berkman Klein Center for Internet & Society, commented, "By 2030, most social situations will be facilitated by bots–intelligent-seeming programs that interact with us in human-like ways. At home, parents will engage skilled bots to help kids with homework and catalyze dinner conversations. At work, bots will run meetings. A bot confidant will be considered essential for psychological well-being, and we'll increasingly turn to such companions for advice ranging from what to wear to whom to marry."[17]

I'm convinced that in the very near future, we will all have a true AI personal digital assistant; one that helps us safeguard our limited attention, time, and, more importantly, our relationships, and has a very positive impact on our human

---

17   "Artificial Intelligence and the Future of Humans," *Pew Research*, accessed October 15, 2020.

condition. This is an example of the thrust forward that will come after the pinch-back we're currently experiencing. Man and machine reciprocally affecting each other's evolution beyond AI: co-evolution.

Questions for Discussion

What do we need to do to bring back the smiles between strangers?

How has smartphone technology impacted your life in a positive way? In a negative way?

Do you feel more disconnected and isolated or do you feel better connected now than you did ten years ago?

What steps could you take today to limit your screen time?

ART AND CULTURE IMPROVING COMMUNITIES

——

"Therefore"
by Bernardo De Urquidi

I feel, therefore I exist,
I think, therefore I am conscious,
I decide, therefore I am free,
I express myself, therefore you know I exist.

What do the words tell you?

¿Cuál fue la fórmula que nos convirtió en lo que somos con todo y nuestras contradicciones? La respuesta es muy simple: en el origen que funda toda comunidad humana conviven la imaginación y la tecnología. No hay edificio sin arcilla ni futuro sin sueños. Si el arte se anticipa para imaginar mundos posibles sus instrumentos los convierten en mundos ciertos y, tal vez mientras el lector llega a este renglón sucede que ha llegado la hora de producir un nuevo diálogo entre el arte y la tecnología, para reconocernos en nuestra memoria, pero sobre todo para entender que el futuro tiene un corazón antiguo: la cultura.

Pablo Raphael

Aeschylus and Plato are remembered today long after the triumphs of Imperial Athens are gone. Dante outlived the ambitions of thirteenth-century Florence. Goethe stands serenely above the politics of Germany, and I am certain that after the dust of centuries has passed over cities, we too will be remembered not for victories or defeats in battle or in politics, but for our contribution to the human spirit.

JOHN F. KENNEDY

Hundreds of programs and organizations are doing a great job of improving communities through arts and culture. Artists who are also entrepreneurs are identifying and developing assets that matter to the people in the communities where they live and work.

Mexico has a very rich artistic tradition that stems from great civilizations like Olmecs, Mayans, and Aztecs that existed long before the arrival of the Spaniards to the "new world." It also has a very rich natural beauty ranging from jungles to deserts, beaches to rivers, and mountains to volcanos. In West Mexico, among multiple mountains of the current state of Guerrero lies a small town named Olinalá. With less than ten thousand inhabitants and a few hours' drive away from Acapulco or Mexico City through narrow and winding roads, it is a secluded area surrounded by green landscapes and blue skies.

Bernardo Rosendo is an artist born in Olinalá who left his hometown to study high school and college at Mexico City and didn't return home for over a decade. Upon graduation, he embarked on a path familiar to many men from his hometown but in very different circumstances. While most of his fellow men traveled to the US to achieve freedom from impoverished conditions, Mr. Rosendo did it on a quest to achieve the freedom to continue developing his artistic skills. While studying at the Art Institute of Chicago and collaborating at an atelier for Mexican artists in the windy city, he also had the opportunity to serve his community being the representative of the folks from Guerrero in Illinois, and later working for the Mexican Foreign Ministry.

In 1995, Mr. Rosendo decided to go back to Olinalá for a year to deepen his artistic knowledge of the *maque*, which is a type of lacquer made with stone powders and oil, compacted through pounding multiple layers of the mix on surfaces, although mainly wood. Then beautifully hand-painted designs are placed on top of it, inspired by the local flora and fauna with vivid colors, as well as silver and gold plates for the most expensive pieces. The more he worked with the local artisans, the clearer it became to him how much the town depended on the artisans and the vicious circle taking place in a vulnerable yet culturally rich society: "The worst was yet to come. The vicious circle in which the artisans don't feel they're being compensated fairly, and the brokers demanding better quality to command a higher price, had become a huge obstacle endangering both the trade, the sustainability of the ancient art, and the community at large. Something different had to be done and right away!" Little did he know that the short stint he had planned would become his life passion and mission.

Unlike the artisans of previous generations with limited exposure outside their towns, Mr. Rosendo had an entrepreneurial spirit and a global vision. He first felt compelled to dig deep into the production process and learn about any changes that had happened to it over time. His teacher was one of the most recognized artisans, Damaso Ayala, and he insisted that the only change had been a gradual substitution of the oil used to mix the powder coming from ground stones. After much effort and frustration, Mr. Rosendo was inspired by one of his findings. Doña Josefa Jimenez, an elder and mother of his teacher, overheard a conversation between them and contradicted his son, indicating that "when I was young, I recall that my dad used to bring the *tezicaltetl* (calcite mineral) by donkey from a place a half-a-day journey away from town. And my mother never bought the powder now being sold to the artisans." Bingo! Mr. Rosendo had uncovered a key change to the process and possibly the culprit of the low quality of the maque.

I couldn't possibly do justice describing the many toils that Mr. Rosendo went through for more than a decade to overcome the challenges he faced to establish an art center—one built as a full program to recover the use of original materials such as the *tezicaltetl* as well as an apprenticeship model to train young artisans willing to use the original process to increase quality. *The Hope in the Mountain* book[18] that he published at the end of 2018 narrates the details of the financial, political, and technical challenges he had to overcome, to sell and implement his vision of artisans creating high-quality works of art that would command a price commensurate with the time and materials it took to create them. Today, he has achieved the cultural rescue and apprenticeship model he envisioned. The art center is a beacon of economic opportunity for the artisans linked to it and the community at large. Mr. Rosendo tirelessly travels within Mexico and internationally to promote the art and artisans of Olinalá, having showcased it at places as far away from his hometown as Spain, Dubai, and China. By doing so, he always generates admiration for the craftsmanship and beauty of the pieces exhibited.

---

18   Bernardo Rosendo, *Esperanza en la Montaña. Rescate Cultural y Formación para el Trabajo* (Mexico: Luna Media Comunicación, 2018).

The crux of the story is that in one of the most impoverished regions of Mexico—further aggravated by being one of the largest producers of opium poppy flowers in the world, a base for heroin production—an artist and entrepreneur was able to identify key assets of his community. He put together a team and worked really hard to gain the trust of the vast majority of the community, to turn the vicious cycle that he encountered into a virtuous one.

In November 2019, I traveled to Olinalá to attend a family reunion and to have a follow-up session on a pilot program to bring technology jobs to young adults in conjunction with Mr. Rosendo. I couldn't believe my good fortune when we got to listen to Gianluca Littera, a famous Italian harmonicist, play the love theme of *Cinema Paradiso* at an event he attended as a guest of the Philharmonic Orchestra of Acapulco, the first time a philharmonic orchestra played in town given its small population.

Cinema Paradiso is by far my favorite movie.[19] What are the odds? I must have watched it at least ten times (twenty if you ask my wife). The main plot takes place in a small Sicilian town a few years after the second world war. Alfredo, one of the main characters, is a middle-aged film projectionist who almost loses his life and ends up permanently blind after a reel of nitrate film explodes in his face. A few years after the accident, he is having a conversation with his friend Toto, the main character who incidentally saved his life, and tells him, "Progress always arrives late," referring to the more modern film that was non-flammable and therefore no longer

---

19   Giuseppe Tornatore, dir., *Cinema Paradiso*, Les Films Ariane, 1988.

caught fire. I've always wondered whether progress always arrives late.

Once the concert was over and I had recovered my breath, the image of Alfredo came to my mind saying, "Progress always arrives late," as did a phrase from the science-fiction writer William Gibson who once said, "The future is already here. It's just not evenly distributed."[20] This is precisely the case in town and in the surrounding villages. An optic fiber connection arrived in town only in March of that year to the central office of the single service provider Telmex/Telcel. Broadband internet access, a legal right in Scandinavian countries, is still very limited in Olinalá and the surrounding villages, and with it a further limitation for the vast majority of the population in access to education and "future" services such as telemedicine.

The Return on Investment from Arts and Culture

In downtown San Francisco, a public park was named after a plant that used to be so abundant in the area that the settlement bore its name. The current name for the city was changed from Yerba Buena only after present-day California was annexed by the US as a result of the Mexican-American War.

The Yerba Buena garden was born from a quest to attract developers to an area of the city victim to postindustrial decay. The Yerba Buena Center for the Arts (YBCA) opened

20 Tim Chatterton and Georgia Newmarch, "The Future Is Already Here— It's Just Not Very Evenly Distributed," *ACM Interactions*, March/ April 2017.

in the fall of 1993 and imagined itself as a new kind of art center—an inclusive center for the people that would prioritize diverse perspectives and experiences, as well as nurture the local art ecosystem. It doesn't have a permanent collection, so it has significant resources that are flexible enough to be put toward building a robust community program that includes performance art, films, and events that complement their temporary exhibitions.

From the Federal Reserve Bank of San Francisco's Community Development Innovation Review:

Today, YBCA embraces its role as a civic institution with a mission to generate culture that leads to individual and societal movement. Inspired by Jeff Chang—author (*Can't Stop Won't Stop*, *Who We Be* and *We Gon' Be Alright*), vice president of Narrative, Arts, and Culture at Race Forward, and YBCA board member—we believe that culture precedes policy and cultural movement catalyzes lasting change. We are committed to creating a place for people to come together to grapple with the urgent challenges and questions of our time. Recent lines of inquiry at YBCA have been shaped around such questions as: Can we design freedom? What does equity look like? How might we reimagine political power? By design, YBCA fellows and artists tackle those questions from diverse perspectives and disciplines, creating a powerful array of nuanced, poetic, out-of-the-box responses. We look for the game-changing ideas—whether they are policy propositions, artistic proposals, or new ventures—and we find a way to incubate them, to make them real.[21]

Has the YBCA improved San Francisco? There is no doubt that it is a leading institution of the nonprofit arts and culture sector in the Bay area, and according to the Arts and Economic Prosperity study published in 2017, the sector "generates $1.45 billion in total economic activity. This spending—$780.6 million by nonprofit arts and cultural organizations and an additional $667.7 million in event-related spending by their audiences—supports 39,699 full-time equivalent jobs, generates $1.0 billion in household income to local residents, and delivers $131.1 million in local and state government revenue. This economic impact study sends a strong signal that when we support the arts, we not only enhance our quality of life, but we also invest in the City and County of San Francisco's economic well-being."

I attended an event in February 2020 where Deborah Cullinan, CEO of YBCA, was a panelist. Here's a highlight of her remarks:

YBCA is trying to transform the paradigm completely. And what we're striving to be is a forum for art and social change. We also are a think tank or an institute that's working on national projects that have the potential to transform our field. And a lot of what we are trying to do is help build awareness about the essential role that artists and art play in any social

21   Deborah Cullinan, "CultureBank: A Vision for a New Investment System," *Federal Reserve Bank of San Francisco Community Development Innovation Review 2019-2*, page 183.

change effort. And we have lots of examples of how we've done that from working with the San Francisco planning department to really shift the culture of planning in our city to the project that is headed up by Penelope Douglas called CultureBank.

CultureBank really understands and positions artists as essential early-stage investors in their communities. And we think that artists are uniquely situated to see and lift and develop assets that matter to people. And you heard it today, from all the artists that we have the great honor of working with, that these are things like language skills, green spaces in our community, intergenerational knowledge—the things that make us alive and rich. And what we see is that people read that signal wrong and invest on top of it. So that is the opposite of the true act of community development investment. And what we're striving for is the kind of investment that is driven by artists in communities where the community is empowered to develop assets that matter to them. And that is what we invest in.[22]

Many artists and entrepreneurs who work toward cultural change and advancement work at a community level, not at a city level. And with their work, they impact cities and counties. One such artist and entrepreneur is Fred Villanueva. He co-founded Ash Studios along with Darryl Ratcliff in 2012.

---

22 HowlRound Theatre Commons, "Arts Culture & Community Investment – Culturebank Dallas with IgniteArts Dallas," February 25, 2020, video, 2:56:00.

Ash Studios is a creative response to the racial segregation, political disenfranchisement, and economic displacement that is the reality for many citizens in Dallas, Texas. Especially, minorities in the East and South parts of the city. Its mission is to encourage interracial and intergenerational dialogue and collaborations between creatives and citizens, to empower creatives to have a voice in public life, and to promote and create opportunities for economic self-determination for creatives.

I interviewed Mr. Villanueva in September 2020, a culture worker in his own words, and he shared that Ash Studios has already impacted over ten thousand citizens and creatives. Despite this success, he still recognizes that the quantitative metrics aren't as easy to track when success starts with convincing a few artists to get involved with their local community to make it a better place beyond the evident beautification. Through education, community building, and community organizing, which is an important artistic form of expression, they "broaden the understanding of what art can be, and also the hope of what it can do, and how it can change people."

Mr. Villanueva has a unique blend of artistic abilities and vision, coupled with an understanding of the business environment. He has worked in corporate America, and as an artist, he has exhibited across the US from California to New York, as well as Spain and The Netherlands. He also has a unique personality because he's friendly, yet when discussing ideas that he's passionate about, turns into a warrior challenging the status quo—a combination that caused him to leave the Cistercian school in Irving, Texas but still maintain a good relationship with the monks to the present day.

"Changing an entire city is an overwhelming expectation. Success really comes down to the butterfly effect: Convincing one person through your actions, getting that individual to get engaged with the community, and that person convincing another one. One becomes two, then two becomes four, four becomes eight ..." Following this line of thought of the multiplier effect, he believes that investment must get directly to the artists to achieve it. Small investments by institutions, cities, municipalities, and states have pretty long-reaching effects. For example, a three-thousand-dollar grant made available to twenty artists lets them empower at least another twenty persons in their communities. That is why he was a strong and vocal advocate for the city of Dallas to establish a micro-grant program. And after four years, it became a reality in 2016.

Mr. Villanueva gave a great example tied to Ash Studios being selected as one of six initial Ignite/Arts Dallas Community Development grants. The funds for the six enterprises were provided by Ignite/Arts Dallas as part of its 2018 Meadows Prize, awarded in May 2019 to CultureBank to establish a unique investment model in Dallas to support artistic projects that benefit the community. Ash Studios' Outdoor Painting Program "built a mirror wall, and by word of mouth, we were recommended to a neighborhood association. This association brought a new piece of art to the Oak Cliff neighborhood with permission from the Texas Department of Transportation and the City of Dallas, representing a forty-thousand-dollar investment. A year later, I'm still watching the dust settle and the seed investment becomes a mural business that will continue to generate jobs. None of that would have happened without that micro-investment from CultureBank."

Investors flock to wherever they can find good returns on investments. San Francisco, California boomed with the gold rush of 1849 thanks to this effect. Capital markets have evolved significantly, making it easier to find good returns, and it's not a secret that investing in arts has been an area overlooked by investors. Impact investing, which encompasses investors seeking social good in addition to financial returns, is shining a bright light on artist entrepreneurs and their work with arts and culture to unlock the potential of human capital in their communities.

Questions for Discussion

How can we expand the investment in the arts to ALL disadvantaged urban and rural communities?

Can you think of a community in particular that you would like to work with?

What natural pairings of communities and art projects can you think of?

What art studios in your community could you talk to about partnering with youth and young adults?

3

SMARTPHONES, SOCIAL MEDIA, AND GEN Zs

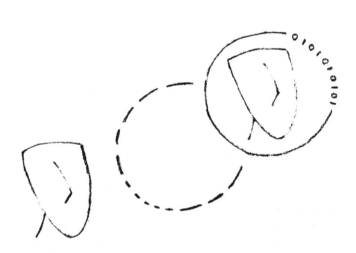

Does the image convey a sense of evolution to you?

Most likely, anyone reading this is familiar with the story of Steve Jobs' life and the way he related to people. In particular, the contentious father-daughter relationship with his daughter Lisa. If he had a better relationship with her, could he have applied his genius to steer the iPhone design in a different direction? For example, in the second part of his career, he dressed almost exclusively in jeans, tennis shoes, and a black turtleneck to simplify his decision-making while getting dressed. Would a better relationship with his daughter have resulted in a heightened focus on how his product could provide a simpler life for youth in light of the technological changes he knew were fast approaching? Would the world be any different today as a result?

Dr. Jean M. Twenge, author of more than 140 scientific publications and books, wrote an article in 2017 titled "Have Smartphones Destroyed a Generation?" published in The Atlantic.[23] In it she writes that "... the twin rise of the smartphone and social media has caused an earthquake of a magnitude we've not seen in a very long time, if ever. There is compelling evidence that the devices we've placed in young people's hands are having profound effects on their lives—and making them seriously unhappy." Why?

Adolescents today are not much different from in the past. The environment has changed from a multitude of perspectives: social, economic, political, technological; yet the struggles remain the same. From a biology standpoint, it takes multiple generations for our physical and cognitive abilities to evolve, and no information or communication technology is going to change that. Now we know, thanks to magnetic resonance imaging scans, that adolescent brains differ from adult brains in two key aspects: Their limbic system, which,

---

23   Jean M. Twenge, "Have Smartphones Destroyed a Generation?" *The Atlantic,* September 2017.

among other things, processes emotions, is more sensitive and gives them more rewarding feelings for risk-taking. Their prefrontal cortex, which helps us control impulses, is not yet fully developed. These are very important facts because they help us put in context the response from adolescents to the changes to their environments over the years.

At the risk of oversimplifying, there have been two industrial revolutions before the information age at the end of the twentieth century and the slingshot effect of the twenty-first century.

The first Industrial Revolution peaked in the early nineteenth century and resulted in the industry dominating a previously agrarian economy. The US had solidified its independence from the British empire and started its expansion. Mexico was struggling as a brand-new country having just gained its independence from the first global empire, the Spanish Monarchy, which was in clear decline. Society started a move to urban areas and the formation of a "middle class." It was the last leg of the Enlightenment period, also known as the Age of Reason. Our current public education system is a direct result of this period. The growth of the capitalist engine demanded a trained workforce and the establishment of a public education system that didn't exist before. It served its purpose well. The shift away from an agrarian society and laws making education compulsory resulted in young people spending more time at school. Adolescents started gaining more freedom from manual labor and from spending time at home with family.

The Second Industrial Revolution is associated with the expansion of electricity, railroads, the automobile, and the arrival of television. Here, the US and Mexico move at very different speeds. While by the mid-twentieth century, 90 percent of rural homes in the US had electricity, Mexico was nowhere close to that.[24] The US had come to dominate the automobile industry thanks to its mass production techniques and cheap labor. Mexico was nowhere close to that. Few people in the US had black-and-white TV sets at home. Mexico had just inaugurated the first commercial TV broadcasting channel in all of Latin America. The Mexican Guillermo Gonzalez Camarena filed his color TV patent in both the US and Mexico in 1941.[25] Society in the US was impacted by the Second World War, the birth of baby boomers, and the start of desegregation. In Mexico, the single dominant political party had been firmly established and would rule until the year 2000. Society was a witness to the "Mexican Miracle," where, thanks to the vast riches in natural resources, a continued expansion was fueled by industry and a surge in births equivalent to the baby boomers in the US. Both countries saw a demographic surge during a time of peace and prosperity, and the automobile gave adolescents more freedom from supervision than their parents or previous generations had enjoyed.

The year 1968 deserves a special note because of widespread student protests across the US, Mexico, France, and many other nations. The baby boomers were the first generation

---

24   Erin Blakemore, "These Women Taught Depression-Era Americans to Use Electricity," History.com, March 29, 2018.

25   Chromoscopic Adapter for Television Equipment Patent US2296019A filed by Guillermo Gonzalez Camarena on August 14, 1941.

to grow up with TVs in their homes and had easier access at scale to news about other countries. While the student protests had different triggers, they also shared some commonalities—namely a counterculture movement and a boomer generation that was more educated, had more leisure time, and questioned traditions and authority.

The post-war economic growth coupled with family planning through the legal use of contraceptives, most notably "the pill," resulted in adult boomers having fewer children and more money spent per child. The consolidation of mass media, which had started with broadcast radio, solidified and multiplied its impact with the additional appeal to our visual sense. Adolescents started being called teenagers to identify them as an addressable market segment that became highly profitable because they were sharing the disposable income of their parents as well as making money on their own. Teenagers continued to gain more freedom from supervision and more leisure time.

Then came the Information Age with the arrival of the computer, mobile communications, and the internet at the end of the twentieth century. A movie released in 2015 opens with an interview that the Australian Broadcasting Corporation did with the science fiction writer Sir Arthur C. Clarke in 1974.[26] Sir Arthur was born in Britain in 1917, and he cowrote the screenplay for one of the most influential films of all time, 1968's *2001: A Space Odyssey*.[27] Remember Hal (one of the most famous computers of all time)? The interview,

---

26   Danny Boyle, dir., *Steve Jobs,* Universal Pictures, 2015.

27   Stanley Kubrick, dir., *2001: A Space Odyssey,* Metro-Goldwyn-Mayer, 1968.

filmed in black and white, shows Sir Arthur in a computer room with a reporter who brought his young son with him, Jonathan. Picture a very big computer room because it took place almost fifty years ago. The camera zooms in on Jonathan, and Sir Arthur states that when he grows up, he will have in his own house a computer not as big as the one in the background but "at least a console to which he can talk to his friendly local computer and get all the information needs for his everyday life."

Not even Sir Arthur imagined back then that we would have such powerful computers on our pockets or wrists. Any smartphone on the market today has the computing power of all the computing equipment in the room where that interview took place, and far better connectivity.

The reporter asks, "I wonder what sort of life would it be in social terms? I mean, if our whole life is built around the computer, do we become a computer-dependent society?"

Sir Arthur replies, making the case for the positive impact that computers will have, "in some ways, but they'll also enrich our society because it'll make it possible for us to live anywhere we like. Any businessman and executive could live almost anywhere on Earth and so do his business through a device like this. And this is a wonderful thing. It means we won't have to be stuck in cities. We could live anywhere, in the countryside or wherever we please, and still carry on interaction with human beings as well as with other computers."

I think that Steve Jobs was looking at the world with glasses similar to the ones of Sir Arthur when leading the design of the iPhone. Both were passionate about the advances in technology and its upside. Did he ever ask himself or had someone in his immediate circle ask the question posed by the reporter: "Do we become a computer-dependent society?"

In his last recorded message, published in 2007, just shy of his ninetieth birthday, Sir Arthur stated that "the world's mobile phone coverage recently passed 50 percent, or 3.3 billion subscriptions. This was achieved in just a little over a quarter century. Since the first cellular network was set up, the mobile phone has revolutionized human communications and is turning humanity into an endlessly chattering global family. What does this mean for us as a species? Communication technologies are necessary, but not sufficient for us humans to get along with each other. This is why we still have many disputes and conflicts in the world. Technology tools help us to gather and disseminate information, but we also need qualities like tolerance and compassion to achieve a greater understanding between peoples and nations. I have great faith and optimism as a guiding principle, if only because it offers us the opportunity of creating a self-fulfilling prophecy. So I hope that we've learned something from the most barbaric century in history: the twentieth. I would like to see us overcome our tribal divisions and begin to think and act as if we're one family."[28]

---

28 *TVEAPFilms*, "The Last Public Message Recorded by Sir Arthur C. Clarke," circa 2009, video. 9:1.

Sir Arthur didn't get to see the rise of smartphones and broadband access that enable ubiquitous connectivity. We have all sorts of information and media available at our fingertips twenty-four seven, and they run the gamut from instruction to entertainment, and from inspirational to indoctrination. The difference between TV and the internet is that the former is a one-way mass media communication method from a few to millions, and the latter allows for targeted and distributed communication. Smartphones have effectively replaced automobiles as the technology of choice for young adults, and with them, they've become overexposed to media and information. Teenagers brandish smartphones as status symbols latched onto apps and social media, further increasing their overexposure and, with it, their anxiety levels.

The term "social media" started being used at the end of the twentieth century, right around the time when the first Gen Zs were born. Not long after the year 2000, *TIME* magazine was circulating with "You" as Person of the Year for the rise in the production of user-generated content, which is a foundation of the social media term as we understand it today: the sharing of information and ideas with virtual communities.[29]

Sharing information and ideas with virtual communities is very powerful and can be used for good. There are great examples of how society can leverage social media to mobilize, and one that comes to my mind is the September 19, 2017 earthquake in Mexico City. Thirty-two years after the earthquake that devastated Mexico City in 1985, on the exact same day, the city was shaken again, causing panic among millions

---

29   YOU, "Person of the Year," *TIME magazine*, December 25, 2006.

of "chilangos" (slang for residents of Mexico City) who, given the anniversary, had the previous earthquake fresh in their memories. Using the hashtags #Sismo19S, #FuerzaMéxico, and #AyudaSismo mainly on Twitter, Facebook, Instagram, and Snapchat, citizens responded immediately to the tragedy. This included checking in with family and friends, organizing volunteers, and setting up shelters and distribution centers for food and supplies. This was all in stark contrast to 1985, where citizens had to rely mostly on government entities for information before they could spring into action.

A challenge with social media networks is that we don't pay for their use. Who wouldn't take advantage of a "free" service? Free anything has a strong pull. However, they're not free because they're for-profit enterprises legitimately seeking to make a return for their investors. That is why they've become advertisement engines relying on our data to sell their advertising capabilities to corporations. The corporations benefit from the ability to directly target individuals for their products or services—not unlike radio or television, yet in a much more precise way, recording and measuring our interaction with advertisements. The social media platforms are incentivized to maximize the time users spend on their platforms. It's an arms race for our attention enabled in the first place by the features, mobility, and connectivity of smartphones.

Long gone are the days when we had to wait to watch our favorite television program on a given day and time or drive to a video rental facility. Nowadays, we have access to any content on demand. Multiple video platforms and video streaming services are racing for our attention. They generate content ranging from educational to entertainment, and they have recommendation engines based on machine learning and AI that serve us more content in a deliberate way to keep our eyes glued to multiple screens of all sizes. They compete with social media platforms, with our relationships, and with our sleep.

Tristan Harris is a former design ethicist at Google and founder of the Center for Humane Technology. He is very vocal about having been part of a control room shaping the thoughts and feelings of internet users. In his TED Talk titled "How a Handful of Tech Companies Control Billions of Minds Every Day,"[30] he presents a simple yet powerful notion: "The only form of ethical persuasion that exists is when the goals of the persuader are aligned with the goals of the persuadee, and that involves questioning big things like the business model of advertising."

We are at a severe disadvantage when faced against control rooms staffed with bright minds and technologies designed to shape our thoughts and feelings. Furthermore, teenage limbic systems are fertile ground for the reward systems of likes or streaks to take hold and become addictive.

In September 2020, I interviewed Dr. Pavica Sheldon and Dr. James M. Honeycutt, coauthors of the book *The Dark Side of Social Media* published in 2019.[31] Dr. Sheldon has been studying social media since she was a PhD student, which

---

30 TED, "How a Handful of Tech Companies Control Billions of Minds Every Day | Tristan Harris," July 28, 2017, video, 17:00.

31 Pavica Sheldon and James M. Honeycutt, *The Dark Side of Social Media* (San Diego: Elsevier, 2019).

coincided with the time when Facebook started to become popular. There aren't too many academics like her, clearly focused on the motives and reasons why users make use of social media platforms. She told me that her first study was on why people use Facebook. She developed the scale for the motives for Facebook use—a scale included in the American Psychological Association database that has been cited close to a thousand times. I asked Dr. Sheldon for her point of view on social norms followed by young adults (see Chapter 5 for more detail on social norms), and she responded: "Teenagers need reassurance because, for them, it's all about social comparison. Based on a study that I performed with teenagers and their use of Instagram, the result was excessive reassurance-seeking and addiction, which led me to write the book on the dark side of social media."

Excessive reassurance-seeking, as well as the conclusion of the first chapter of their book, are to be taken very seriously: "Studies show a negative influence of social media on one's mental and physical health. In general, the more time someone spends with social media, the more stressed, anxious, or depressed he or she is. This is especially true for adolescent and passive users [browsing others' profiles without posting their own material]. Participants who more frequently reported using social media were more likely to report sleep interruptions by their devices. Another problem is social media addiction. Personality traits, Fear of Missing Out (FOMO), and stimulating content contribute to social media addiction. Detrimental outcomes include mental distress, decrease in the quality of interpersonal relationships, and declining school or work performance. More research is needed to understand the full scope of social media impact on mental and physical health."

Interestingly enough, mobile communications represent a backlash in terms of freedom for teenagers because parents have come to expect to have constant communication with their sons and daughters. And this is an important fact because that backlash was balanced by teenagers gaining more freedom in a space their parents couldn't quite control: cyberspace. This shift resulted in teenagers spending more time on connected devices, whether they be computers, tablets, gaming systems, or smartphones. Gen Zs are the first generation to grow up with smartphones and social media.

Gen Zs are tribal and have evolved for tribalism. Much like previous generations, they have to learn how to develop the social skills they need to succeed. Physical interaction is absolutely necessary to develop them. Dr. Twenge wrote in the aforementioned article that "adolescence is a key time for developing social skills; as teens spend less time with their friends face-to-face, they have fewer opportunities to practice them. In the next decade, we may see more adults who know just the right emoji for a situation, but not the right facial expression."[32]

A key insight from the 2016 Global Millennial Viewpoints Survey indicates that mental health care needs to be prioritized worldwide for youth to meet their potential, and found particularly concerning that of the 56 percent of the youth

---

32   Jean M. Twenge, "Have Smartphones Destroyed a Generation?" *The Atlantic,* September 2017.

surveyed, there was a 50/50 ratio of sixteen to nineteen-year-olds and twenty to twenty-four-year-olds, saying, "The way I feel gets in the way of my studies, job, or social life."[33] The age ranges of the youth surveyed places most of them in the Gen Z category. Furthermore, 45 percent agreed with mental health care being one of their top three most urgent healthcare needs, and 16 percent agreed with mental health being their most urgent healthcare need.

We are putting Gen Zs under a perfect storm of isolation, noise, and distraction while asking them to focus and make difficult choices.

Questions for Discussion

Do you think that social media companies will regulate themselves? Will governments regulate them, or must we act as a society to regulate them?

Have you seen evidence of social media affecting your mood or emotions? Or those in your family?

What steps could you take to decrease the time you spend on social media?

What can you offer to a community or group that will provide a hands-on experience not centered around their smartphone?

---

33 "2016 Global Millennial Viewpoints Survey," International Youth Foundation, accessed October 15, 2020.

4

ART AND EDUCATION

—

What jumps at you from the sketch?

I find the story of my friend and business partner Nicolas Gonzalez to be one of hope and inspiration for millions of voiceless young adults who are hungry for role models they can relate to and will allow them to visualize opportunities in life. It also acts as an inspiration to change society's approach to education in this twenty-first century.

In February 2020, Mr. Gonzalez inaugurated a mural painting at the Mexican Consulate in his hometown. The inaugural address is given by the highest government official representing Mexico in North Texas, Consul Francisco 'Paco' de la Torre. Witnessing the unveiling and with an expression of awe on his face is Judge Clay Jenkins of Dallas County. I see Nic nervously awaiting his turn to address the attendees and among them those most important to him: his family. It has been two months since he was commissioned to paint the mural, yet it has been fourteen years since he communicated to his parents that he would be an artist. Unlike the celebration that often takes place when kids tell their parents that they want to become engineers, Nic's news was received with disapproval from his dad.

Mr. Gonzalez spent countless hours on his indoor mural inspired by the twentieth-century movement in Mexico that was started by internationally well-known names such as David Alfaro Siqueiros and Diego Rivera. On it, he portrayed his dad and his niece. Through his talent, he captured a magnificent social portrait. A river cuts across not only two countries, but through generations of a family that is representative of a significant thread of the social fabric of North America. On the right hand, a migrant whose aged hands continue to help build one of the most powerful nations in the world. On the left is his granddaughter wearing a graduation cap and overlooking the farmland that he manages still to this day. The grandfather was born in a country that couldn't provide enough opportunities for him to capitalize on his entrepreneurial spirit, hard work ethic, and long-term investor perspective—an individual willing to forego short-term returns to ensure the success of generations to come. Don Isaías wasn't afforded an education to obtain the skills sought after by enterprises in his native Mexico or the US, so along with his wife, he took a high risk and migrated to the land of opportunity. All the Gonzalez family thank Doña Maria and Don Isaías for their sacrifices. Mr. Gonzalez was grateful to have all of them witnessing one of his accomplishments.

Mr. Gonzalez is the youngest of three siblings, each of whom is a "product of growing up in a rough neighborhood." Yet unlike his brother and sister, he was born with a gift for drawing that helped him overcome the anxiety he frequently felt while attending public schools in an underprivileged part of the city—schools that are part of an educational system not well-adapted for him or, for that matter, any other kid who didn't conform to a norm established by administrators who didn't understand Nic's culture or personal needs. Even though there were not enough computers available in the overcrowded schools he attended, Mr. Gonzalez became technologically literate thanks to his dad buying him a basic personal computer and being one of the first kids in his circle of friends and many cousins to have a cell phone. Nic fondly recalls being an early dial-up internet user when he discovered that he could download songs patiently over a number of days and burn CDs. His gadgets and, more importantly, his sharing them with peers, helped balance his introverted personality. Learning from his older siblings' mistakes kept him out of trouble. His artistic abilities and doing just enough in a failed system helped him graduate early from a high school that felt like a "prison" to him. Experiencing manual labor in the roofing and janitorial areas was also a strong incentive for him to pursue higher education.

Being the first one in his family to graduate from high school made him feel proud yet confronted him with a stark reality: He had no knowledge of the process nor did he have the support to apply for college. His early graduation earned him a scholarship to Eastfield Community College, so he took it—a new environment, one with no cameras on every corner or metal bars on the windows. *Free at last*, he thought, only to find out that he was totally unprepared for the academic challenge. He felt discouraged and dropped out. "Welcome back" was the message waiting for him among his neighborhood peers who were glad to see Nic join their "fun," which is what Mr. Gonzalez did for a while.

Arts and Large-Scale Assessments

"Every student that drops out of school has a reason for it, which is rooted in its own biography. They may find it boring, they may find it irrelevant, they may find that it's at odds with the life they live outside of school. There are trends but the stories are always unique."

— SIR KEN ROBINSON, BRITISH AUTHOR, SPEAKER, AND INTERNATIONAL ADVISOR ON EDUCATION.[34]

I believe that Sir Ken Robinson would agree with Luis Camnitzer because for the former: "Education is a creative profession and not a delivery system."[35]

In my opinion, standardized tests or large-scale assessments are a key element of educational systems behaving more like a delivery system than what they should be.

---

34 *TED*, "How to Escape Education's Death Valley | Sir Ken Robinson," May 10, 2013, video, 19:11.

35 Luis Camnitzer, *Visiting Minds 2013: Radical Pedagogy* (Panama: Sarigua. 2013).

Recent decades saw a significant increase in the use of large-scale assessments (LSAs) in education. More LSAs have been developed and implemented. More students and teachers have been subject to the consequences of LSAs. More countries and areas have engaged with LSAs. As a result, the impact and influence of LSAs have become broader, deeper, and more consequential.[36]

LSAs have been used for a variety of purposes. The chief among them are three: Accountability, selection, and comparison. LSAs for accountability are assessments intended to hold educational professionals accountable for their students learning. The US, for example, has been using statewide LSAs to hold teachers and school leaders accountable for student achievement through legislations such as the No Child Left Behind Act.[37]

If LSAs could measure all that is desirable in education and what matters in life, they would serve as an excellent tool to improve education. However, it is impossible for LSAs to measure everything that matters in education and for individual success and societal prosperity for several reasons.

- There is much dispute over knowledge, skills, and other human qualities that make a person successful

36 Trina E. Emler et al, "Side Effects of Large-Scale Assessments in Education," *ECNU Review of Education* 2, no. 3, September 2019, pages 279–96.
37 Ibid.

in life or a society prosperous in the future as human societies are constantly changing.

- We do not have valid and reliable ways to assess many important human qualities such as creativity, entrepreneurship, and social and emotional well-being on a large scale.
- The uniform nature makes it difficult for one LSA to validly and reliably measure everything that matters because what matters can be in conflict or competing with each other.
  - The high costs make it difficult to develop and administer unlimited numbers of LSAs frequently. For these reasons, LSAs have only been able to measure skills and knowledge in a very limited number of areas, such as mathematics, language, and science. What has been measured is typically limited to cognitive ability in these areas.

The growth of LSAs suggests their value and utility in education. LSAs can be powerful tools to hold educators accountable, efficient means to collect and provide evidence for policy making, and are perceived as objective and incorruptible instruments for sorting and selecting individuals for competitive opportunities, such as prestigious colleges. Accompanying the growth in use and impact is the growth in criticism of LSAs. While LSA has never lacked criticism, its growth has attracted more.[38]

---

38 Trina E. Emler et al, "Side Effects of Large-Scale Assessments in Education," *ECNU Review of Education* 2, no. 3, September 2019, pages 279–96.

The Power of Alternative Education Programs

Sir Robinson has talked about alternative education programs, and he's indicated that successful ones have certain common features:[39]

- Personalization
- Strong support for the teachers
- Close links with the community
- Broad and diverse curriculum
- Often programs that involve students outside of school as well as inside

David J. Sullivan is an awesome individual who has been serving his community since 1977. He developed his servant leader character and commitment to the community thanks to his mom and dad, who were Catholic missionaries in New Mexico, Kansas City, and Belize. His father was an optometrist and psychologist who gave up his private practice in Holyoke, Massachusetts and became the first white doctor to work at the Samuel Rodgers Clinic that primarily served African Americans and Hispanic patients in Kansas City. Dave worked for the DeLaSalle Education Center, an alternative school, from 1977–1998. Dave then founded ArtsTech with the mission to better the lives of underserved urban youth through the development of artistic, technical, health, and educational skills.

---

39   *TED*, "How to Escape Education's Death Valley | Sir Ken Robinson," May 10, 2013, video, 19:11.

I learned about ArtsTech from Deborah Cullinan, and in July 2020, I drove from Dallas to Kansas City to meet Mr. Sullivan. It was a long drive; however, in the midst of the COVID-19 pandemic, I felt safer in my vehicle than flying. Since I met Dave, we have held several conversations, which have always been energizing. It is also inspiring given his clear vision of successful alternative school programs, both from a theoretical standpoint and in the results that his organization has achieved for thousands of young adults. Mr. Sullivan fully agrees with Sir Robinson and highlighted the service component involving students outside of school.

Dave gave me a great example of this service component: "ArtsTech has been performing digital inclusion work since its founding. Recently, we operated an intergenerational project that trained fifteen high-school-age youth to be neighborhood Digital Connectors to reach 250 senior citizens. The young adults participated in a forty-hour training program where they learned twelve core competencies, including digital literacy. Upon completion of the training, they were certified by the instructor. The Digital Connectors then used their new technology skills to teach 250 senior citizens basic internet, email, and Photoshop skills in a ten-hour training session. We not only taught digital literacy skills to youth and senior citizens. We changed their lives!"

Back to the arts' side, Mr. Sullivan stated, "Art makes a positive difference in troubled young people's lives" and recalled the case of Cicely—a confused, bitter, and disruptive teenager who had been put out of three schools before attending ArtsTech. Art helped Cicely achieve significant academic and mental health improvement. Art proved therapeutic and provided the healing that Cicely needed.

Another feature of alternative education programs that Mr. Sullivan highlighted was the personalization, which he called Individualized Instruction. It cannot only be part of alternative education; it has to be part of mainstream education.

The central element of a competent education system is the student. And when our twenty-first century demands lifelong learning due to the change in the nature of jobs, the mindset of the student becomes even more relevant. Any education system must consider how to develop a successful mindset in the learner if it's not already present.

I had the privilege of being introduced to Sixto Cancel at the end of 2015. His story is one of determination and pain transformed into purpose. On the premise that all young people deserve to thrive despite adversity, he founded a nonprofit that focuses on leveraging technology to change the foster care system and achieve better outcomes for youth aging out. He was no stranger to the foster care system, having entered himself at eleven months old. He grew up in it except for a one-year period when he was about six years old and returned to his biological mother, only to go back into the system. Adopted at age nine, couch surfing at thirteen, and re-entering the system by fifteen, Mr. Cancel knew he was living in a dysfunctional and broken system. He's made public before that he even suffered physical and verbal abuse by an adoptive mother who trained him on "what happens in this house stays in this house." Once during a conversation with a social worker, he stated that they didn't suffer any abuse, yet when she asked him whether he went outside to play, he candidly responded: "No. We can't do that." Mr. Cancel was doing a good job of covering up and doing exactly what his adoptive mother was telling him to do. He just didn't know at the time that those things weren't normal. Unlike other young adults in his situation, he developed an awareness of not having to accept it.

The low performance of his school teachers who lost their temper, weren't trained on de-escalation, and weren't using innovative practices to teach, gave him the sense that there had to be something better. He had to prove the abuse committed by his adoptive mother, only to be dismissed by the system on a technicality. It turns out that she was unaware of being recorded. This made Mr. Cancel realize he had no voice and gave him the freedom to gain his voice to advocate for himself. His constant complaining to social workers gave him a ticket to the youth advisory board where he started advocating for others in his shoes.

I was able to interview Mr. Cancel in June 2020. He was busy as usual, and we had to make the most of the limited time we had scheduled, so we dove right into how he developed that awareness: "The fifteen-year-old me got involved in musical theater thanks to a teacher who took it upon herself to bring this group of fifteen young people together after school; not as part of any school program, but on her own and without funding. She was fully committed to it and to making a difference, even picking us up on her van or coordinating parents to do it. We would show up at the same place and put on plays as well as see plays that helped me gain perspective. One such play was about a freed slave trying to buy his wife's freedom. That stood out for me and had an ever-lasting impact."

His theater teacher would be one of many mentors that Mr. Cancel has had throughout his life, and to this day, he keeps in touch with her and the group gets together for a Christmas gathering. In his own words: "Throughout life, I've had a lot of different mentors, and at each stage of your life your relationship with them changes. It's important to always be open to how the relationship will feel different as you go through these different stages. I'm here because of my mentors. It's priceless and critical to have the ability to pick up the phone to call three or four folks and be able to rely on them and their feedback when making difficult choices. Connect with supportive adults or people that want to be there for you."

The determination in his character is reflected in his posture and his eyes as he goes on to explain the concept of setting high performance expectations for him and others, something he learned upon entering the Clinton Global Initiative University and seeing firsthand what true innovative action looks like at a higher level. He talked about young people his age using data and technology to really have an impact in the world: "That set the table for me. There are all these things that are broken and don't work well. I should do something about it, and being exposed to high performing functional initiatives is the way to do it."

Mr. Cancel is a firm believer in the power of technology as evidenced by the focus of his organization, yet when at a point in our conversation he mentioned "these things" that young adults should figure out and learn, I requested that he expand on what he meant by "these things." He stated that he was referring to "how to regulate your emotions. How to communicate with other people. How to work with other people. How to form your dreams and thoughts. How do you want to spend your time beyond surviving?"

Mr. Cancel doesn't believe that we can live in a world where we only communicate virtually. We need to have in-person experiences, and that should never be taken completely off the table. When interacting with young adults, we must listen to understand what their own healing journey is. What is their own development journey and what development tree works for each one of them? We should engage much more of the arts and in-person programs. The system is flawed in that we see these things as interventions because the youth are lacking something, when in fact, they're supposed to be learning. They are supposed to be figuring things out and learning as they go.

He also believes that we need to truly understand all diversity of opinions because we're getting to the point where people are intolerant of people's individuality. For him, "Theater is one of the strongest forms of actually putting on a character and trying to understand a lot of that character back and forth."

Someone that would fully agree with Mr. Cancel's view is a drama teacher who taught for thirty-two years at Miami Beach Senior High School and considered Mexico City his second home, Jay W. Jensen. His students have included well-known actors such as Andy Garcia. A documentary titled "Class Act," released in 2007, highlights the importance of arts education in the public school system.[40] It incorporates multiple golden nuggets that are aligned with the story of this inspiring and dedicated high school drama teacher.

The Arts: Secondary or Not

In an interview, Dr. Elliot W. Eisner, one of the leading academic minds in the US, states: "I think the justification of the arts on the basis of non-artistic outcomes is a dangerous line of argument for the arts, because it really indicates that what matters are math scores, and the arts are handmaidens to mathematics."[41]

I once believed that math scores were one of the most important indicators of the progress of students, and that the teaching of music helps improve those scores. However, I now think differently, and I'm in full agreement that the arts stand on their own and, when intersected with technology, offer a very powerful education combination.

Alfie Kohn, author and lecturer in the areas of education, parenting, and human behavior, states in this documentary: "I guess what bugs me most is the idea that arts are a means to something else. I think I am going to scream if I hear one more person say music is good for kids and that it raises their math scores. You know, just once I'd like to hear somebody say the reverse. You know, we should give kids a little bit of math because they can become so much better musicians and artists. In that case, I mean hell, the arts stand or fall on their

40   Sara Sackner, dir., *Jay W. Jensen and the Future of Arts Education in America,* Sackner Films Inc. 2007.

41   Ibid.

own, and they need to stand. They enrich our spirits. They ennoble our existence. They're not instrumental to improving skills in some other arena."[42]

Dana Gioia is an internationally acclaimed poet and writer whose mother was Mexican and was born in Los Angeles. For fifteen years, he worked as a businessman before quitting at forty-one to become a full-time writer. He is the former Chairman of the National Endowment for the Arts. In this documentary, he indicates multiple things that are even more relevant today than when it was released:

> It's hard to measure the state of arts education objectively, and I say this with some regret. There do not seem to be any fully competent national measures of this that we can statistically sort of read what's been happening over the last twenty years. But I think that the local evidence and the qualitative evidence is pretty straightforward. Arts education seems to be declining across the United States, the sorts of things that we used to be able to take for granted. High school instruction in band, in chorus, theater programs, and dance being incorporated into physical education are really dropping away in a lot of the country. So you have a generation of kids who are coming to maturity without the advantages of arts education.[43] ...

> I think this is quite dangerous, and I'll tell you why. If you think about high school, it comes to the point

---

42 Ibid.

43 Sara Sackner, dir. *Jay W. Jensen and the future of arts education in America*. Sackner Films Inc. 2007.

where kids are essentially finding their adult identity. What is their place in the world? Now, there are very few paths to success as academics, and a certain number of kids will succeed in academics. There are sports. A certain number of kids will intensify themselves and their identity, build their self-esteem, do sports maybe in addition to academics. But a lot of kids are not good in academics or in sports or are kind of mediocre in those, and what art education does is provide another alternative to self-discovery, to building self-esteem, and also to understanding your own talents. And I've seen this in my own experience as a teacher; if you create a possibility for a kid to do well at something, suddenly they tune into that class in a way that they simply don't otherwise.[44]

And so you have a position where the worst kid in your class, the class clown, suddenly becomes the class star because you've made the recitation of Shakespeare, recitation of poetry, or acting as part of the curriculum rather than simply analytical study. And so I worry that by losing arts education, we're losing a significant portion of the next generation. These are going to be kids that don't really match up with their talents. That don't discover what they're best at.[45]

And if this country is going to compete with the rest of the world in the twenty-first century, it's not going to be from cheap labor; it's not going to be from cheap

---

44 Ibid.
45 Ibid.

raw materials; it's going to be from creativity, ingenuity, and innovation. A nation which does not invest in arts education is not going to have those capacities at an elite level for the future.[46]

I don't believe the decision is primarily a financial one. This country has had an enormous capacity in the past to find ways of doing what it knows needs to be done. I think the problem in America is the sense that this is a secondary or tertiary priority. Arts tend to be the first thing that get cut in budgets and tends to be the last thing to be reinstated. We need to convince people that this is fundamental to the development of students to providing adequate education in a free market, democracy, and to really making this country competitive in the twenty-first century. If people realize that, the funding would not be an issue.[47]

What worries me about American education, and God knows there's a lot that worries me about American education, is that we're somehow settling on saying that the purpose of public education is to produce minimally skilled entry-level workers for society. That is not the purpose of education, especially in a democracy. The purpose of education is to produce young adults who are capable of leading full lives economically, culturally, personally, and politically in a democracy. And that's what we should be aiming at.[48]

---

46   Ibid.

47   Ibid.

48   Sara Sackner, dir., *Jay W. Jensen and the Future of Arts Education in America*. Sackner Films Inc. 2007.

One more reason I find this documentary even more relevant is that it was released before smartphones and social media became popular. It will stand as a point of reference for the future, and to that extent, one particular quote caught my attention.

"This country is dividing into two groups, one which is literate, active, and engaged—people that manage their own time and make room for everything in their lives. And a second group of people who have a very passive relationship to electronic media. They watch TV, they fiddle around the internet, and they play video games. They're not reading, and if you can't read, the arts are largely closed off to you," states Dana Gioia.[49]

Art is important to develop curiosity, collaboration, and communication, as well as creative and critical thinking as key twenty-first-century skills.

---

49   Ibid.

Questions for Discussion

If the education institution that you are attending, or that your children are attending, doesn't offer an arts program, will you seek one?

Is there an extracurricular arts program that you could propose to a local school? Who would you need to help you with this?

What steps could you take as a community member to let school board members know about the importance of arts in the schools?

5

GEN Zs: YOU DIDN'T INVENT DISRUPTION

Neolithic Symbols

The only constant is change. Yet some
things don't change much. Do they?

Young adults might not know that in Mexico, rock concerts were banned by the government for almost two decades. In 1971, a large-scale rock concert took place in a small town located two hours away from Mexico City, Avandaro, similar to the famous Woodstock concert of 1969 in the US. As a result, being a young adult not thriving under the traditional education system became synonymous with being a felon with a communist mind, challenging family values and social peace. Therefore, the Mexican government banned concerts to tame the rebellious and oppositional attitude of young adults.[50]

In both the US and Mexico, the beginning of the modern teenage culture started after the Second World War. Adolescents were mostly busy performing manual labor at farms or in the cities before that period of economic and population growth. The 1960s was a period of significant social change: long hair, psychedelic drugs, student protests, and the generational gap started widening. Then came the 1970s, where young adults rode on the shoulders of the teenage freedoms gained in the previous decades.

Maria Elisa Wolffer, a teenager in the 1980s, grew up in Mexico City's Coyoacan neighborhood not far from the Frida Kahlo Museum. She was educated to question the status quo and value people for who they are and not for what they have. She identifies herself as a disruptor and out-of-the-box thinker. Her "traditional" education path ended early. She

---

50 Canal22, "Documental 1968-1971, Los Jefes del Rock," May 14, 2009, video, 49:3.

became a serial entrepreneur and then a full-time mom, raising her three children at Queretaro in central Mexico.

I can see confidence and determination in the way she's looking at me while recounting that she spent her elementary and junior high school years at private schools and became a rebellious teen. She entered a junior high school chosen for her by her parents, and as she grew up, she wasn't happy at all, particularly with how materialistic her peers were. One day at a public student gathering in her freshman year of high school, the principal asked all students whether anyone wasn't happy at school. She mustered the courage to stand up in front of everyone and raised her hand, thinking: *Since my parents don't listen to me, then I hope the principal will.* As a result, her parents were called to the school and allowed her to transfer to a school of her choice closer to home.

Her new school was much laxer academically, and she cruised through her sophomore and junior years. She realized that she wasn't happy at the new school she had chosen either because she wasn't learning much, other than how to play dominos, which she recounts with a grin that she can't hide. She transferred to a third high school to rejoin several of her childhood friends and graduated. She started college at the School of Management of Institutions, a private college focused on the hospitality industry, because she was passionate about cooking and service. In her first semester, she was already struggling academically and on top of it entered into a very heated discussion with a teacher, so she was expelled. Her father had had enough of her rebellious attitude and told her she had to start working or she would be kicked out of the house. She joined the Fuddruckers hamburger restaurant and waited tables.

In her own words, she could have ended up in prison in her teen years and, fortunately, didn't. When I asked what kept her from it, she gave me an unexpected answer: "I have always had good vision, intuition for character in people, and an ability to be a connector. Plus, I've always had great alignment of mind, heart, and gut. I'm very sensitive, and when meeting someone new, I focus on vibes. If I sense a negative vibe, then I walk away. My antenna is always up and scanning."

She thinks she got the sensitivity from her grandmother—who wasn't educated yet was wise—and her father, who was a fan of music and instilled the love for it in her. She took music lessons from a very young age and much like her dad, cannot function without music: "I could tell whether my dad was home or not by listening to whether music was being played or not. He would always have music playing in the background."

A gift from her dad that she remembers fondly is a boombox she received when she was thirteen. She also loved spending time listening to concerts with him, whether live or recorded. Not surprisingly, the first thing she does when working is to put music on, selecting the type of music to go along with the task at hand, which means she can have a range of music accompanying her—from Mozart to eighties' rock or "grupero" music.

I found it very easy to connect with Mrs. Wolffer even though I had only briefly spoken with her once before our interview. She tells me it's what happens to her all the time, and frequently people ask her for advice. Her advice to young adults like her three children is: "Make sure that you first and foremost connect with yourself. Everyone has at least one ability, and your task is to identify what makes you feel good. Then figure out how you can stand out by using it to be productive and earn a living."

If you're a Gen X or Millennial, you can likely relate to Mrs. Wolffer's story even if you grew up in the United States. If you're a Gen Z, there might be some foreign concepts such as a boombox; however, you can likely identify with rebel teen or disruptor attitudes.

I had a conversation with Tyler Durman in July 2020. Tyler is the author of *Counterintuitive. What 4 Million Teenagers Wish We Knew (Bite-Sized Wisdom 4 Parents and Teachers.*[51] He has spoken to more than four million teenagers over the course of thirty years. Following each presentation, invariably teens approach him to confide and confess things they've never told their parents, teachers, or even best friends. He knows teenagers in and out.

I want to contrast Mrs. Wolffer's experience with that of teenagers' described by Mr. Durman's expertise in the topic, to show how struggles haven't changed across generations. Can you relate the struggles that you've faced, or are still facing, with the ones that Mrs. Wolffer experienced, even if she belongs to a different generation than yours?

---

51 Tyler Durman. *Counterintuitive. What 4 Million Teenagers Wish We Knew (Bite-Sized Wisdom 4 Parents and Teachers).* (Laguna Beach, California: BSWisdom Books, 2015).

Can you sense some arrogance in Mrs. Wolffer's rebel teen story? Mr. Durman told me: "Young people are always arrogant because they always think they're smarter than the old people. There's a lot of truth to the old saying youth is wasted on the young. Their worldview is that people above a certain age don't have anything to contribute because we don't understand."

Professor Sarah-Jayne Blakemore, award-winning author of *Inventing Ourselves: The Secret Life of the Teenage Brain* indicates that "adolescence is associated with changes in behaviors. Behaviors like risk taking and impulsivity and peer influence peak in adolescence. These behavior changes are consistent across species, across cultures, and also across historical descriptions of adolescence. It is a period of life where we're forging our own identities and, particularly, our sense of social self—that is, how other people see us. It's where adolescents start off with very chaotic social hierarchies and they have to form peer groups."[52]

Peer groups of adolescents are no different than peer groups of adults in that their behavior is governed by unwritten rules or guidelines, called social norms. These social norms specify what is acceptable and what is not acceptable in the group. Furthermore, there are two types of norms: What we're supposed to do (injunctive norms) and what everyone else is doing (descriptive norms). Add the element of perception of those social norms, and you can see that it gets very complicated very fast. Good communication and trust are

---

52   *TED*, "The Mysterious Workings of the Adolescent Brain – Sarah-Jayne Blakemore," June 1, 2013, video,14:26.

very important to have a shot at understanding the social norms of other groups.

Mr. Durman stated, referring to young adults:

> They need to know that we value them. It's all about listening—true, empathetic listening and seeing them and spending five to twelve minutes a day. If we can give them the opportunity to share something about their day, little or big, even if they don't feel like sharing, they notice the intention. And all those things add together to say to this young adult: I see you and I value you. I'm busy; I'm stressed. But you matter to me.
>
> Every rebellious kid I've ever met wants desperately to be close to their parents. They want that more than anything because they're like BBQ chicken; they're not done on the inside even though they seem to be. I give them a small strategy of how they can go home and what they can do to get their parents to take a second look at them and see their hearts. And I just give them a very simple strategy—tell the truth. And I think it's pretty powerful in its simplicity yet changes their whole demeanor and attitude. All I do through this strategy is give them hope that they can affect the outcome of their life.

Just like some struggles haven't changed, new ones have emerged, and Mr. Durman shared that young adults growing up in this digital world that we now live in are living in a fake world that feels real to them. And what's lost in terms of wisdom and connection to the world beyond the screen is huge. He went on to give a couple of examples.

> Young people see their experience of humanity through the eyes of performance in a way they've never done before. And it started ramping up in my purview when social media kicked in. In fact, my wife and I were in Hawaii last year, and we went out for a romantic night. We were on a balcony and looking at the ocean. On the next level of the balcony below us was this mom and these four preteen girls who, for forty-five minutes, did nothing to experience the environment. They just used it as a backdrop to their pictures. And they would take pictures of each other and then rush over to look at the screen. And then you see them posting on social media or they do selfies. And they missed out on the experience of the beauty of where they were standing because they're so focused on 'how am I going to be perceived?' Their world becomes a function of how it can cater to their performance and how people perceive them as opposed to life becoming a delicious thing to struggle through and to enjoy.

We all know about addiction; we know about anxiety. With teenagers, it's higher than it's ever been. Suicide is higher. In my school, if a kid made fun of me, I'd come home and wouldn't think about him until I walked into school the next day. Well, with social media, that's not the way it is. It's twenty-four seven, and it increases the amount of stress kids are under.

A few years ago, a school asked me to visit them because they didn't know how to handle what was going on with their kids and social media. One of the cases was about four girls. You wouldn't look at them and think they were bullies. These four girls targeted a fifth girl that they didn't like. And they would take videos of the fifth girl and make fun of her, her hair, her nose. They were real personal attacks, and then they would post them on social media. I learned that it wasn't their ultimate goal. Their goal was to provoke a confrontation to start a girl fight; a fistfight the other three girls would record to post on social media. It's this whole perverse, twisted way to see the world.

Mr. Durman made a statement that really resonated: "Love is not digital." Our advanced technologies present many advantages to keep us connected across long distances or physical barriers such as the ones imposed by the "social distancing" and mandatory lockdowns that happened throughout the world during the COVID-19 pandemic.

> Young adults think you can build a relationship digitally through texting, but you can't. You need to see facial expressions, reactions . . . Young adults are so lonely because this isn't a real human connection.

> Smartphones serve a great purpose. I'm a car guy and I love tools, and my iPhone is the best tool I've ever had. But I like to sit around and not look at my phone. Whereas I've got a lot of friends and peers my age who, the second there's a commercial or they're waiting for the waiter, immediately check their phones. I want

to take in life. I want to experience it as it comes. My Hawaii background really has taught me about that. And I think screens really get in the way. I'm producing a video series for parents to watch with young teenagers called "Love is Not." And it's a list of things that our culture thinks love is, but it's not.

An interesting study confirmed that assessing the impact of an individual's social network on an individual is difficult without administering a large number of surveys. However, online social networks with built-in data collection circumvent this problem.[53] The same study also found that people's perceptions of social norms are a strong predictor of healthy and risky behaviors. If we were to demand social media platforms to find a way to use the data they collect on each individual to assess the positive or negative impact on any individual's social network, we could disrupt the disruptors. Or better yet, a smart innovator could design a true personal digital assistant (PDA) to do that precise task for each and every one of us—a PDA that helps us safeguard our limited attention, time, and more importantly, our relationships, having a very positive impact on our human condition.

I see social norms and the perception of them changing at breakneck speeds. The gaps within generations keep widening. I find it difficult for me as a parent of Gen Zs, and my parents who are loving and wise find it next to impossible to keep up. Gen Zs: You didn't invent disruption. You

---

53   Christopher J. Carpenter, Amaravadi S. Chandra, "A Big Data Approach to Assessing the Impact of Social Norms: Reporting One's Exercise to a Social Media Audience," *Communication Research* 46, no. 2 (March 2019): pages 236–49.

are disruptors like young adults before you and that's okay. However, unlike previous generations, you are also being disrupted. You more-than-older generations are being disrupted and rolled over by technology. And this is contributing to the increased number of disoriented individuals among your peers and across baby boomers, Gen Xers, and millennials.

Questions for Discussion

Gen Zs: what behavioral changes will improve the outcome of your lives and your families' lives?

Gen Zs and non-Gen Zs: whose responsibility is it to close the generational gaps?

What steps can you take to decrease the gap between generations?

What's one thing you wish your parents/grandparents knew about you? If you're a parent, what's one thing you wish your Gen Z child knew about you?

6

SUCCESS VS.
SUCCESS MINDSET

Please take a moment to write something with a pen or pencil on a piece of paper. Not on your smartphone, tablet, or any other electronic device. Feel the pencil scratching the surface of the paper...

"Not having given myself life,
I will not deprive myself of it,
as long as it demands something fine of me."

What do you think about this idea written by Napoleon Bonaparte while on exile at the isle of Elba after having had one of the most successful military and public administration careers know to western culture?

This particular idea from Napoleon Bonaparte was recorded by a wise mind of the eighteenth century on his *Memoirs from Beyond the Grave* by Francois de Chateaubriand.[54] There's also a quote attributed to him that I believe is still very relevant: "Presumably, the human species will grow in stature and volume, but it is to be feared that man, as an individual, will decline; certain eminent powers of genius will be lost; and thus imagination, poetry, and the arts are endangered in the cells of a highly developed society, in which each individual will be nothing more than a bee, a machine gear, an atom of organized matter."

Angelica Mosqueda, a wise young adult who is part of a re-engagement program, the NXT Level Youth Opportunity Center in San Antonio, was put down often as a kid. She faced challenges in her family environment, has a leg injury that keeps her from doing many things she would like to do, battled depression, and despite still having nights where she "just can't function," recently graduated from high school. She loves to read, particularly mystery novels. She plans to continue her education in the criminology and justice field, so she's uniquely positioned to help us solve the mysteries that both adults and young adults face.

I asked Ms. Mosqueda how she picked up reading. Her mind wandered to when she was a kid and her energetic voice stepped up a notch: "I was barely starting pre-K, and while riding in the car with my mom and cousin, we would play a little game where they would have me read the signs of the storage wheel that we drove by. When I got to third grade, it

---

54   Francois De Chateaubriand, *Memoirs from Beyond the Grave* (1849-1850).

was around the time we started standardized testing, and I honestly did horrible at math. But when it came to reading, I remember it was fifty questions on that test, and I missed only one out of the fifty. I got forty-nine out of fifty. I remember that score to this day! From then on, reading just came naturally to me. I would always score high on the Scholastic Reading Inventory and would always be above my grade level when it came to reading evaluations. By the time I was in middle school I was reading at a college level."

She went on to tell me how close she was to her mom while growing up and how at some point, after her late elementary school years, they stopped communicating as well as they should have and kind of grew apart. Her parents separated around that time, and she stayed with her mom. This was a traumatic event for her because she didn't understand what was going on and the communication gap with her mother widened. Her mom became ill and then passed away less than a month after her sixteenth birthday: "I remember the night before she passed. I was crying because I was so scared. And I even prayed, saying, 'Dear God don't take her away from me. I'm not ready to say goodbye.' The next morning it was just like reality had kicked me in the stomach, and I felt like something was taken from me that shouldn't have been. I figured I would have closure after the funeral, but it just kept getting worse for me. I couldn't function. I couldn't sleep. I didn't want to eat. I hardly talked to my friends, and when I was by myself that's when I really broke down. The first day I went back to school after my mom's funeral, I broke down crying. They called my dad to come get me. I just completely broke down. I couldn't function anymore. I felt like a ghost, like I was a shell. I just had to learn how to deal with it because I didn't want people to worry about me. I didn't want anybody to worry. What helped me a great deal is that I had many friends that were there for me when I needed them. I felt like I wasn't alone and that helped me a lot."

Her last statement brought my mind back to the isolation part of the perfect storm that I described. I asked Ms. Mosqueda her thoughts on young adults who do have access to a resource network even if it's not evident to them, yet they don't take advantage of it. Ms. Mosqueda replied, "Don't just rely on yourself. It's not easy when it's just you. You need that person, a family member, a teacher, counselor, even a significant other, depending on your age. You need somebody who can say, 'Here's what we can do to help you.' Don't miss the chance because you never know when that can be taken from you. And I think people in general, kids of this generation, rely too much on technology. And it makes me sad. When I was in high school, we had a library and not a lot of people were going. They relied too much on the iPads that were issued to us. But what if that technology failed? How else would you get your resources, your literature?"

She took a deep breath and switched gears: "Don't let your friends or your family suffer alone. Let them know you're there. Ask them, 'If you needed help, why didn't you tell me?' If you see someone having trouble, struggling with whatever, be there. Be that person to lean on. Let them know you know they're not alone. Reassure them, because I've been through that as well and with everything going on at the time, I was not tough enough not to crack. It was hard for me to get through, even with therapy and then even with joining the NXT Level program. I was hesitant at first because I was scared but I did have a friend that got through to me and said, 'You need this,' so he got me to join the program. He kept reassuring me. Reassurance is one of the most beautiful things there is because it lets the person know that they're not alone. It's one of the most beautiful things I've seen when friends are there for other people who are just going through hard times. If you see somebody having trouble. Go ask them."

I am positive that you will enjoy reading through the following stories of individuals with successful mindsets, and through it, you will gain a better understanding of what success means to *you* in a way that is conducive to feel appreciated and cared for as a member of a group of people that you are close to or want to be close to, even if you make a really bad mistake.

Ana-Maria Ramos is a state representative of the great state of Texas. She grew up in the southern part of Dallas, Texas in a simple working-class family of Mexican immigrants who didn't have higher education. She was the middle child of seven, and no one in Mrs. Ramos' family had ever graduated from college by the time she dropped out of high school. She didn't know what higher education meant because it wasn't something that anybody really ever talked about in her environment. When she dropped out of high school, it was just normal and natural for her to do it. Fast forward and Mrs. Ramos not only completed her GED after becoming a teen mom, but she also went on to obtain her associate degree from Eastfield Community College and later graduated from the University of Texas in Arlington. She obtained her MBA from Texas Woman's University and capped her education with a law degree from SMU. What an amazing turnaround.

I asked Mrs. Ramos whether there was something that sparked her mindset change. Her radiant smile no longer as visible, she replied it was her daughter. Her husband and she were barely making it back when their baby was born. She explained: "Unfortunately, and I say unfortunately because it had to come to that, it really was. I do tell the story that I knew poverty. I tasted poverty, even worse than when I was growing up. Because now I was the one responsible and I didn't want her to experience what I had experienced. I didn't want her to be in Parkland Hospital with eight other women in a room. I didn't want her to be a mom at fifteen in South Dallas like I was. I didn't want her to have to take the bus like I did just to get basic prenatal care and be treated as an inferior. I didn't want her to be in line for food stamps, which is what I was doing. So I knew that I had to do something different." With her radiant smile back, she added that her grandfather was also a factor by showing her his GED diploma. Her grandparents immigrated from Mexico in the 1950s and spoke no English. Back then, he couldn't have possibly taken the exam in Spanish. Seeing what her grandfather had achieved made her realize that if he had done it, then she could do it too. It was the moment that got her going and when she realized that things were going to get better. She could have greater opportunities if she just kept going.

She recalled the education "thing" she had seen on TV and white people becoming doctors and such, so she told her abuelita: "I want to go back to school to further my education!"

Her abuelita, who had nine kids, replied, "Mija, you already had a baby, and your body now requires you to keep having babies for the rest of your life." Mrs. Ramos tells me her grandmother was a beautiful person, and she understood her response was based on her culture. Her abuelita became a key figure, fully supporting her in her pursuit of higher education as well as all her future endeavors until she passed away.

She recounts with sparkles in her eyes how her family taught her hard work, resourcefulness, and being creative. She tells me, "You're always very resourceful if your AC is not working while growing up. When you don't have central AC and it's burning outside, then you put your chair next to the wall unit. Or you jump in the shower for two seconds, get wet, and run around the neighborhood wet. And that's how you cool down."

She loves to dance cumbias, and journaling has helped her a lot. She definitely considers writing as a form of artwork. It's how she can be creative and express feelings and emotions. She went through some really tough times when she dropped out, and writing was an escape for her. Journaling has allowed her to go back and track her growth and progression toward her goals and uses it to this day.

Nowadays, as a state representative, she continues to teach government at El Centro Community College because she became passionate about education and is a firm believer in preparing young adults to take over the work she is doing. Civic engagement and the Constitution are subjects that she teaches her students, mostly black and brown kids, and for years, they have talked about protest songs. She has a lecture that has just been the most amazing lecture where she connects with her students through music and teaches them that the First Amendment is about freedom of speech.

She also teaches how music is not just a form of art, but it's also a form of civic engagement and exercising your first amendment right.

She plays Bruce Springsteen's "Born in the USA," and they go through all the lyrics and how that is a protest song against the war in Vietnam. And then they go through the 2 Live Crew's "Banned in the USA." She encourages her students to bring her their favorite protest songs as well and express what it says to them and how they protest through it. She has listened to music from Africa, Indonesia, and even Vietnamese hip-hop. She recalls that one time a student asked her whether the song could be in Spanish. Mrs. Ramos replied, "Absolutely," and after the student discussed her assignment with her abuelitos, they suggested that she bring the "Somos Mas Americanos (We're More American)" song from the Mexican-American band Los Tigres del Norte. Her black students were surprised to discover that Texas and California were once part of Mexico through her class.

Mrs. Ramos tells me: "To be able to connect the Constitution and the freedom of speech with music for eighteen- and nineteen-year-olds is so powerful. It is so rich because our young are impressive. They're watching, they hear you, they see if you're fake or not, and they have so much to say." She recalls having things to say yet nobody asking her. She wasn't heard as a student, and she knows that her students want and deserve to be heard. Her students have many barriers in their lives just like she did, and she knows that there's always a little crack in those barriers. She's convinced that it's our job as adults to practice creative ways to find those cracks, to get through to them, and listen. "There's always one little thing they'll say to you that allows you to ask more questions. And the gems you find are surprising!"

Now a story from Mexico. Arturo Velez is a professional who bridges creativity with technology. His work has allowed him to interface with most countries in Latin America. He also connected with multiple Asian countries while living in China for a couple of years on an international assignment. He dropped out of high school one year before graduating because he faced a perfect storm. He was frustrated with the bureaucracy of how credits were managed at his school. He also remembers "not knowing what I wanted to be when I grew up. I had so many interests. One day I wanted to follow in my father's footsteps as a doctor, the next I wanted to pursue a career in finance only to change again the following day. I vividly remember meeting with the vocational counselor and feeling even more confused. He kept presenting me with alternatives when all I wanted was for him to help me make a choice." Meanwhile, his job as a teen software programmer was starting to take off. He hasn't looked back.

He was born and raised in Mexico City, the son of a doctor and a young mother who obtained her high school diploma once Mr. Velez and his younger sister no longer demanded her full attention. He gained access to technology when he was seven or eight years old thanks to the family gifting his dad with one of the first personal computers (PC) available on the Mexican market. He combined his fascination with the PC with the interest in learning that he observed while his mother studied for the equivalent of the GED exam in the US.

It is clear where Mr. Velez's technical skills come from. Less clear were the origins of his creativity. I specifically asked him about it, and he replied, "My love for soccer was eclipsed by the fun I would have discovering on my own about how the Atari PC functioned. I would follow a BASIC language programming book for kids by copying instructions into the computer, and I marveled at the output of my work by immediately seeing results on a cathodic ray monitor (CRT). I enjoyed the play dates with the PC and my imagination when I came back home from school. In addition, my dad was an amateur carpenter, and we would spend time wood-working to build furniture for our home. I also recall how my younger sister built *alebrijes* (animal-like figurines that are carved and painted)."

"Early in my professional life, I was very fortunate to join a small team at a company in the nascent multimedia and web development industry. I was able to collaborate with creatives who were almost a decade older than me and were super smart. None of them had college degrees, by the way. In addition to aiding them with creating video animations, we would do very cool stuff like interface with large advertising agencies or develop text masks for the TV broadcasts of *Telehit*; the Mexican equivalent of Music Television (MTV) in the US. The bonds I formed with them eventually led me to be pulled into a team of what became the now leading digital innovation studio in Latin America: Naranya. Those bonds led me to a sixteen-year career there. I sometimes miss the great corporate culture. What I don't miss is my former coworkers because we truly became a family and we still hang out with each other."

He went on to recount how his understanding of technology and creativity enabled his entrepreneurial spirit: "When I started high school, I began to freelance by helping others with PowerPoint presentations and tutoring them on Microsoft Office. I posted flyers in the neighborhood to repair computers as well. My mom took notice of my small ventures and started introducing me to friends of hers that had corporate jobs. They wanted to outsource the preparation of PowerPoint presentations. I would use my creative skills to enhance the color schemes and prepare animations by leveraging the lesser-known features of the software, which was relatively new back then."

Mr. Velez, throughout his career, has seen an infinite number of both individuals and business models fail and succeed. His advice is "to learn about mindfulness and emotional intelligence. Strengthen your mental flexibility. Learn to play with different thoughts and entertain your mind with ideas and points of view from others. Learn to meditate and practice regularly. Sometimes we are our worst enemy when we start doubting ourselves, or by keeping stuck with unproductive thoughts. As humans, we can choose to control and master our mind and, with it, our own success."

Has anyone told you that you will not succeed? That you will never be successful? That you're destined to be a failure? Some people hear it more than others. Some people say it more than others. I find that success is a big word that is ill-defined, and the same goes for the word failure. Are they linked? Is the absence of success the same thing as failure? The origins of the same words in English and Spanish are different and entered each language at different times hundreds of years ago.

Success has also evolved over time. For our early ancestors' success was as simple as not being eaten. For

To appreciate beauty; to find the best in others; to leave the world a bit better, whether by a healthy child, a garden patch, or a redeemed social condition; to know that even one life has breathed easier because you have lived. This is to have succeeded."[55]

RALPH WALDO EMERSON

I hope that you have gained a better understanding of what success means to *you* in a way that is conducive to feel appreciated and cared for as a member of a group of people that you are close to or want to be close to; despite how many mistakes (no matter how bad) you've made. This is not a self-help chapter or book. There are individuals, community programs, and institutions to provide *you* the support that *you* need. *You* just have to want it and reach out!

Questions for Discussion

How about pulling out a piece of paper and pencil again, and writing down what success means to you?

Do you have a practice that helps you to stay mindful, such as journaling or meditation?

If you were interviewed, what lessons learned would you share?

---

55   The success quote attributed to Ralph Waldo Emerson, who lived in the nineteenth century, could have been an original quote from Bessie Anderson Stanley.

7

ALTERNATIVE PATHS TO COLLEGE

——

Please jot down a few questions ….
Even better if you post them on www.atriskofgreatness.org

Now I'm going to ask you a question: What if
you combine the following statements?

"One of the most important things questioning does is to
enable people to think and act in the face of uncertainty."

with

"You can't control everything that happens to you, but you
can control the amount of effort you put into things."

We all have heard that time is the great equalizer of life because we each have twenty-four hours in a day—no more, no less, regardless of socio-economic status, race, religion, sexual orientation, geographic location, or education level. And I agree. The difference lies in what each of us chooses to do with our own time. Like other assets, time can be invested, wasted, or stolen. Unlike some other resources, time is non-renewable; that is, once it's gone, then it's gone forever. We cannot turn back time.

Any time that we spend on education is definitely an investment that yields a return. The return varies greatly depending on a multitude of factors, not unlike investments in real estate, for example. Most of us believe that unless we possess an extraordinary skill in sports, arts, or entrepreneurship, investing time, energy, and money in furthering our education, and that of our children, will yield the best returns, particularly when taken all the way to a college degree or beyond college into graduate education. I now think differently, and I'm completely against the idea that a college education separates "winners" from "losers."

In this twenty-first century, the advancements in technology, automation, and artificial intelligence are making it abundantly clear that any repetitive task is bound to disappear, and fast. Some experts estimate that up to 85 percent of the jobs that will exist in 2030 have yet to be invented.[56] And to thrive, individuals will have to successfully perform non-routine tasks that require social intelligence, complex critical

---

56   Daniel Tencer, "85% of Jobs That Will Exist in 2030 Haven't Been Invented Yet: Dell," *Huffington Post,* July 14th, 2017.

thinking, and creative problem solving, all key success factors when competing with machines.

The flip side of the same advances of technology have significantly lowered the barriers to access knowledge, knowledge that in the past was only accessible through a college education. And the shift in the education field and its disconnection with the employment structures result in a knowledge economy where another equalizer has surfaced: Intellectual curiosity! The importance of asking the right questions has risen and will only continue to increase.

Ian Leslie, author of *Curious: The Desire to Know and Why Your Future Depends on It*, said in his "Why We Must Continue to Learn and be Curious" lecture: "We're programmed to be curious. We're born with a very powerful instinct that there is stuff we don't know. And we're also born with that instinct that other people are stores of knowledge. Little children are like investigative reporters pumping their sources for knowledge. Researcher Michel Yunard recorded the conversations that families have at home and discovered that between the ages of three and five, children asked forty thousand questions on average. The questions that they asked were specifically explanatory: How and why. The evolutionary reason for this is that we're cultural animals. The way we survive is by becoming part of a cultural vehicle. We realize that we need to learn if we're going to survive. We need to learn a lot, so we ask a lot of questions."[57]

---

57 *RSA (Royal Society for the Encouragement of Arts, Manufactures and Commerce)*, "Ian Leslie on Why We Must Continue to Learn and be Curious," June 18, 2014, video, 19:7.

Curiosity and questions go hand in hand. It is important, however, that the questions we ask are the right ones.

Leslie goes on to say, "Diverse curiosity is the hunger for the new and the novel; it's what makes you click on the flashing link. It's important because it takes us off in new directions. By itself, it can become rather superficial and futile. Epistemic curiosity is what happens when diverse curiosity grows up. When we combine diverse curiosity with effort, self-discipline, and focus, it becomes deeper and more enduring. It's the life-long quest for knowledge, for learning. The desire not just to find answers, but to explore new questions."[58]

In the interest of exploring new questions, the Opportunity Pathways Background Paper from Strada Education Network, a starting framework to reimagine pathways between education and employment, indicates, "Policymakers, philanthropists, and practitioners keep trying to transform American performance on metrics we all agree matter: closing the achievement gap, raising college readiness, expanding college access, and boosting completion. And those measures do matter. But increasingly, those deeply involved in the work of education reform are beginning to ask if we are solving for particular pain points in a disjointed system, rather than focusing efforts on the ultimate goal: creating pathways for economic mobility and life stability for individual Americans."[59]

---

58 RSA (Royal Society for the Encouragement of Arts, Manufactures and Commerce), "Ian Leslie on Why We Must Continue to Learn and be Curious," June 18, 2014, video, 19:7.

59 "Opportunity Pathways Background Paper," Strada Education Network, accessed October 15, 2020.

I briefly served with Amy Dunham on the board of a leading adult mentoring organization based in Indianapolis called Trusted Mentors. I spoke with Mrs. Dunham in February 2020, at which time she was the SVP of Marketing and Communications at Strada Education Network. At one point in our conversation she stated: "We've interviewed 350,000 Americans about their experience with postsecondary education, and one of the things we've asked is what would they have changed about what they studied and what they did. On the advising aspect of their experience—which is key to their sense of the value of their education—one of the things that comes across is: The advice they want most is from employers on what should they be doing to make themselves more attractive for the workforce. But it's the advice to which they have the least access. If the system were more consumer-centric, the paths between education and employment would be many. I think of it in terms of a map of the backcountry of a mountain: You can get from here to there in a lot of different ways. There need to be more options for people to get the education and skills training they need to build meaningful careers, because today's system simply leaves far too many Americans behind."

The system is changing, and in the past decade, there has been a big push for STEM education at all levels as a way to meet the current and future demands of our knowledge economy. In many instances, it is combined with social and emotional learning (SEL). I like Mrs. Dunham's idea of a map of the backcountry road of a mountain and have attempted to sketch it in the following pages.

The intent isn't to create a market analysis of all programs in North America or beyond. It is to provide input for *you* to generate the questions. Each listed program presents a valid path with advantages and prepares young adults to be productive for a job, and in some cases, a career. As usual, there are always tradeoffs. I have grouped them under four broad categories:

- Technical training or apprenticeship programs while in high school, such as the Gilbreath-Reed Career and Technical Center in Garland, Texas. In Mexico, the Job Training Institutes from multiple states (ICAT for the Spanish acronym) coordinated as decentralized entities by an organization under the Ministry of Education.
- Short duration technology training such as General Assembly, Kenzie Academy, Flatiron School, Holberton School, and Hack Reactor in the US. Techbridge in Mexico.
- Corporations training young adults, such as Cloudfactory or Samasource, which cut across national boundaries.
- Programs squarely aimed at reengaging young adults, such as NXT Level and Restore Education in San Antonio. In Mexico, the "Jóvenes Construyendo el Futuro" nationwide program and platform.

The next chapter explores in detail the intersection of arts and technology as an empowering alternative. To close this section, here's the story of D, as I agreed to call him, since he wanted to preserve his anonymity.

D shared with me that he turned very rebellious and even reckless as a preteen. As a teenager, he didn't do much better because he continued challenging authority, cursing teachers, started smoking weed, and his performance at school decreased to the point that he had to drop out during his sophomore year, a "typical" case of a disengaged young adult. He was a heavy user of social media applications like Instagram, Snapchat, and Facebook, which he uses for entertainment. He tells me that he also uses LinkedIn. "LinkedIn?" I ask, thinking I hadn't heard him quite right. He explained to me that his use of the more "professional" application was due to his work experience. He works as a cashier. Making a lot of money is exciting for him, and he figures connecting to others and networking are necessary for him to achieve his goal.

His work as a cashier, which he started with almost no training, frequently exposed him to rude customers. He would wear his emotions on his sleeve and the clients could tell by the look on his face and tone of voice. It wasn't easy for him to control his anger, and sometimes he had to take a break and go to the restroom to breathe and calm down as advised by his coworkers, who would encourage him to not suppress his emotions while balancing it to keep a smile toward clients. He credits that difficult and conscious effort of practicing anger management with him learning to control his anger and maturing over time.

I ask D whether he has any role models, and I can hear his excitement on the other end of the telephone line when very quickly and without hesitation, he replies: "My dad. We don't live together because he has to frequently relocate for work within the US and Mexico, where we have family. My brother and I used to travel in the summer or on holidays to visit him. We particularly enjoy visiting museums with him, which goes well with my interest in history. Actually, at the end of last year, we attended a ballet for the first time, *The Nutcracker*. I really liked it!"

D's story shows how young adults need more quality physical interaction with friends and family. Building trust is critical for effective two-way communication, and as illustrated by D's story, quality trumps quantity when it comes to spending more time "together."

D credits his participation in the NXT Level Youth Opportunity Center in San Antonio's reengagement program with him being close to obtaining his GED and continuing on to pursue a college education. He was also pleasantly surprised by the team managing it: "They are the only people I've met that genuinely care about the community. I wasn't expecting that when I arrived, and I've been very pleasantly surprised." In closing, he asks me to share this with at-risk young adults: "No matter what you've been through, you can accomplish your goals! Always believe in yourself."

The Dallas Federal Reserve Bank published an "Opportunity Youth in Texas" report in October 2019,[60] where gathering qualitative data, three focus groups were conducted with opportunity youth enrolled in a reengagement program. All focus groups were asked what advice they would give to their disconnected peers looking to reconnect, and these are their responses:

---

60   Ana Crockett et al, "Opportunity Youth in Texas," *Federal Reserve Bank of Dallas*, October 2019.

"Speak your mind."

"Don't let anything hold you back."

"Learn from my mistakes."

"Be heard and not listened to."

"No more self-doubt."

"Admit your mistakes."

"You only live once; make good decisions."

"Don't get greedy–stick it out [by completing high school rather than working]."

"Give it [the program] a chance and be open minded."

"Don't give up."

"Work hard."

"Keep going."

"Read a lot."

"You can't control everything that happens to you, but you can control the amount of effort you put into things."

"Don't leave a stone unturned."

I like D's story because once he reengaged, he decided to pursue a college education. I want to be clear that I'm not advising anyone to not pursue a college degree. For millions of young adults, college provides the education that they need for the twenty-first century, even if it doesn't guarantee success in life.

In Mexico, "Less than a quarter of the young population (twenty-five to thirty-four-year-olds) have obtained higher education qualifications, and within this limited share of graduates, evidence shows that their skills are not used effectively."[61] In the US every year, over 1.2 million students drop

---

61 "Higher Education in Mexico: Labour Market Relevance and Outcomes," OECD, accessed October 15, 2020.

out of high school[62] and 56 percent of college students who start a four-year college curriculum do not graduate in four years and end up dropping out by year six."[63]

If you're in this last category or just feel disengaged, my hope is that this book inspires you to reengage.

The Blue-Collar Stigma and Vocational and Educational Training

Bryan Caplan, an economist and author, states, "As a society, we continue to push ever larger numbers of students into ever-higher levels of education. The main effect is not better jobs or greater skill levels, but a credentialist arms race."[64]

In both the US and Mexico, as a result of multiple social, economic, and political factors, the culture has been one of aiming for a college education and, only when not possible, finding an alternative path. There is a blue-collar stigma where folks with a college degree are conferred a higher status than the ones who don't have a degree. And as proof, blue-collar workers who successfully transcend their "cast" into a white-collar job are recognized and praised.

The system worked relatively well during the mid-twentieth century but then started to show some signs of foundational

---

62   "11 Facts about High School Dropout Rates." DoSomething, accessed September 10, 2020.

63   "U.S. College Dropout Rate and Dropout Statistics," CollegeAtlas, Updated June 29, 2018, accessed September 10, 2020.

64   Bryan Caplan, "The World Might Be Better Off Without College for Everyone," *The Atlantic,* January/February 2018.

stress toward the latter part. The advances of automation and AI that are now evident in the twenty-first century have revealed further results of stress because we're now faced with the possibility of not enough jobs, as we know them today, being available in the not too distant future. Yuval Noah Harari, in his book 21 *Lessons for the 21st Century,* shares "… despite the appearance of many new human jobs, we might nevertheless witness the rise of a new useless class. We might actually get the worst of both worlds, suffering simultaneously from high unemployment and a shortage of skilled labor. Many people might share the fate not of nineteenth-century wagon drivers, who switched to driving taxis, but of nineteenth-century horses, who were increasingly pushed out of the job market altogether."[65] This gave rise to the debate surrounding the pros and cons of a universal income concept.

I interviewed Esther Benjamin, who has been working in global development, international education, and youth development for over twenty-five years, and is currently the CEO and Executive Director of World Education Services (WES). WES is a social enterprise focused on global higher education, credentials, and qualifications. I asked whether she sees changes in the model going forward in terms of alternative paths, and her response was unequivocal: "Absolutely. There certainly are alternative paths to college for work and livelihood. While WES is primarily focused on higher education, our social impact and philanthropic programs consider individuals at all educational, skill, and experience levels, to

---

65 Yuval Noah Harari, *21 Lessons for the 21st Century* (New York: Penguin Random House, 2018), page 30.

support people to find meaningful employment opportunities." Commenting further, she added, "Increasingly, life skills are considered substantially by employers, to include organizational skills, problem solving, critical and creative thinking, communication, team, and interpersonal skills." When asked about her success mindset, she noted, "Striving for success is an individualistic endeavor. I focus instead on a contribution mindset, in order to strive to make a difference in society." In terms of her leadership advice, she noted an essential component: "It is so important to be intellectually curious and to ask more questions in order to excel in the workplace, regardless of where one sits in the organization."

A country where the blue-collar stigma doesn't exist is Germany. "In contrast to the US, Germany has a highly effective work-based vocational training system that has won praise around the world. While university graduates in Germany also earn much higher salaries than workers who have attained less education, vocational education, and training (VET), in Germany it is a very common pathway to gain skills and embark on successful careers: 47.2 percent—nearly half—of the German population held a formal vocational qualification in 2016. Fully 1.3 million students in Germany enrolled in VET programs in 2017, compared with only 190,000 individuals who registered for apprenticeship programs in the U.S. in the same year. Less than 5 percent of young Americans currently train as apprentices, and most of them are in the construction sector."[66]

---

66   Ajit Niranjan, "What is Germany's Dual Education System — and Why Do Other Countries Want It?" *Deutsche Welle,* April 6, 2018.

Ralf Hermann, head of the German Office for International Cooperation in Vocational Education and Training (GOVET), has stated that "a system that has grown in Germany under very specific conditions cannot just be exported to another country under very different conditions."[67]

In November 2019, I held a couple of meetings at the Mexican-German Chamber of Commerce and Industry's (CAMEXA) office at Santa Fe in Mexico City. I learned that Mexico is the country outside of Germany where the German-based vocational education and training system or dual education system (Modelo de Formación Dual in Spanish) has yielded the best results. There has been a successful implementation of not only the German dual education model, but a Mexican dual educational model that adapts the essence of the German model to the reality and needs of the Mexican labor force and labor demands from industry. From my meetings, I gathered that the German model has been limited in scope and duration to generate the Mexican model.

"In recent years, a number of new work-based training systems have been developed in various states [in the United States], some of them brought to fruition by German companies.

One such example is the dual training systems that the German companies BMW, Siemens, and Volkswagen, imported to North Carolina, South Carolina, and Tennessee to compensate for the lack of skilled workers in those states. The Volkswagen program was initiated in 2000, while

67   Ann-Cathrin Spees, "Could Germany's Vocational Education and Training System Be a Model for the U.S.?" *World Education News + Reviews,* June 12, 2018.

the programs of Siemens and BMW were established in the late 2000s and early 2010s, respectively. Trainees in these programs receive supervised training at industrial plants, learning skills in areas like mechatronics, mechanical and electrical engineering, or computer software. Trainees study in tandem for associate degrees at local community colleges that have partnered with the companies.

The German companies' financial investments are sizable: They usually pay salaries and tuition, or at least provide tuition assistance. Graduates typically continue their studies in bachelor's programs while being employed at the companies. In Charlotte, South Carolina alone, Siemens reportedly spends a total of $165,000 per trainee. (A detailed overview of these programs is provided by the International Labour Organization.) The programs are supported by the state governments with measures like tax credits for apprenticeship sponsors; they have been so successful in fostering skills development and economic stimulation that other states like Virginia, Maryland, Pennsylvania, Massachusetts, Wisconsin, and Ohio are exploring options to adopt similar apprenticeship programs."[68]

Emmanuel Winkler is a global citizen and Senior Expert in dual vocational training and sustainability. At a conference organized by the Educational Institute of Aguascalientes, a state in central Mexico, he represented CAMEXA and

---

68 Ann-Cathrin Spees, "Could Germany's Vocational Education and Training System Be a Model for the U.S.?" *World Education News + Reviews,* June 12, 2018.

GIZ.[69] In it, he highlighted the role that corporations have in the education of the talent pool, which cannot be simply outsourced to education institutions. Corporations derive a positive return on investment when comparing dual TVET to other onboarding and training mechanisms because it is based on a truly interactive involvement in an integral dual educational model with all actors (companies, chambers of commerce, unions, certifying bodies, state and educational institutions, families, and apprentices). He also highlighted the future of work relying on human capital confirmed by continuous learners and critical thinkers.

Mr. Winkler described how the dual educational model is the backbone of the German, Austrian, and Swiss economy where young adults between the ages of fourteen and eighteen years old, when their rebellious attitude often peaks, find themselves busy and motivated by it, in stark contrast with the traditional educational systems. In one of the multiple conversations I held with him, he stressed that "to ensure continuous learning, we need new forms of education at all levels and comprehensive systems that allow a staggered education."

We're experiencing a shift toward skills-based learning, training, and hiring practices. An article published by the Society for Human Resource Management in 2018 asks hiring managers to think twice about requiring a college degree.[70] Mr.

---

69 Instituto de Educación de Aguascalientes, "Webinar ¿ Quo Vadis - Educatio? - Educación Dual y Formación Profesional Continua - versus Formación clásica Universitaria," July 31, 2020, video, 1:02:00.

70 "How to Adopt Skills-based Hiring Practices," Society for Human Resource Management, accessed October 15, 2020.

Winkler raises a very good question: "In light of the changes that we're facing in this new century, how can we develop a model that combines the flexibility of the US model with the European one which has shown the many advantages of certifications designed and validated by corporations, unions, and the education institutions?"

Advanced technologies open up many alternatives for those with a success mindset and epistemic curiosity. The limitation is no longer geographical, and new pathways are being developed for communities similar to ours all over the globe. When there is no black or white, right or wrong, as is often the case in life, there are always tradeoffs. I encourage you to find your path based on your passion and strengths.

Please jot down a few more questions. I encourage you to start several of them with "What if?" and "What else?"

Questions for Discussion

What companies can you think of that could offer an approach similar to the companies we talked about above—something similar to an apprenticeship?

What else can be offered to students as they graduate high school to make them feel they are going on a career path but does not involve the standard options?

What if your company, or the company you work for, created such an option for young adults? What would that look like?

THE INTERSECTION OF ART AND TECHNOLOGY

How would you represent the intersection of art and technology?

This is it for me.

I'm one more engineer convinced that the STEM fields are necessary in this twenty-first century. I flew next to a rocket scientist once. We struck up a conversation and at some point, we started discussing how carbon was so prevalent in both organic and inorganic matter. We parted ways once we got to our destination, wishing each other a safe and productive trip, and half-jokingly agreeing that in time, in the not too distant future, software could become more prevalent than carbon, software, data, algorithms, machine learning, artificial intelligence. They all require significant knowledge and mastery of the STEM fields.

However, the STEM fields alone are not sufficient when considering the challenges that we are facing in this twenty-first century, and the further acceleration that resulted from the 2020 pandemic. Leonardo Da Vinci, an individual that exemplifies the universal genius, would marvel at our technology and even more so at the access to art that we have at the palm of our hands. Had he been born today, would he have chosen a STEM field or an arts field? I'm confident that just like when he was born in 1452, in the Renaissance period that allowed him to use his insatiable curiosity and bright intellect to the maximum after the Black Death had ravaged Europe, he wouldn't have to choose. He would benefit from a STEAM education as it's known today. That is, adding an A to STEM (the A being for Arts).

I'm confident because I see a movement that's been years in the making. In 2011, Melody Barnes, then Director of the White House Domestic Policy Council, wrote an editorial piece where she touted the release of the "Reinvesting in Arts Education: Winning America's Future Through Creative

Schools" report and clearly indicated, "Education is one of our nation's most important investments. And an education without the arts is incomplete. That means that arts education can't be an afterthought—an investment that our schools can make only after they've solved all the other challenges they face. Instead, we must see it as a tool for keeping students more engaged, for closing achievement gaps and lowering dropout rates."[71]

Also in 2011, an article by John M. Eger titled "National Science Foundation Slowly Turning STEM to STEAM" appeared in the *Huffington Post*.[72] The operative word is *slowly*. It has been slow; however, the time is right for it to gain speed and achieve scale. Why? There are multiple ways to achieve the intersection of arts and technology, as well as an increasing number of organizations, people, and entrepreneurs dedicated to it.

I am among those entrepreneurs and I joined forces with Nicolas Gonzalez, the artist whose story I've highlighted in this book, and Adriana de Urquidi to found Kosmos—a social venture at the intersection of art, technology, and opportunity—an opportunity for the millions of disengaged young adults in the US and Mexico. We want to be a leading force in the movement to achieve scale because we are passionate about the outcomes that will be achieved and the

---

71 "Reinvesting in Arts Education: Winning America's Future Through Creative Schools," Obama Whitehouse Archives blog, accessed October 15, 2020.

72 John M. Eger, "National Science Foundation Slowly Turning STEM to STEAM," *The Huffington Post*, May 31, 2011.

change that will be unlocked. A description of The Kosmos way, our response to this need, is found later in this book.

A STEAM pioneer in the United States is Education Unbound founded by Rowayda Shoujah Hamdan (aka Weeda) and her husband Mark Hamdan in 2016. Mrs. Hamdan is an artist whose story of resilience and passion for education is amazing and parallels Mr. Hamdan's. I interviewed her in September 2020, and even though I already knew parts of her story, I was still blown away when I heard her recount how she went from being born in West Africa to Lebanese parents, to living in Lebanon during the Israeli invasion of 1982, to fleeing to Europe and, ultimately, coming to the United States.

Mrs. Hamdan is at her home studio, and I get a glimpse of paintings that range from work in progress to finished works of art. She is articulate and energetic yet conveys a strong Zen feeling, that is until she started recounting her life in closed quarters during the war. Her eyes become teary and she pauses a bit as if to muster the strength needed to face those memories again. Visibly emotional, she recounts how "having lived through multiple wars in Lebanon, my family and I have been displaced repeatedly. If it weren't for the warm and welcoming homes of distant strangers, my family's fate would have been fraught with tragedy."

She continues, "It's 1982, and I'm sitting upright, cross-legged, a sketch pad and pencil on my lap with complete darkness around me, my family members propped against each other. Cold, concrete walls. The hopeful waiting has now turned into the heavy reality—we aren't sleeping in our beds tonight."

"Days and nights pass. Our underground bunker becomes our security as battles rage over our heads. On one of those many, nondescript nights of waiting, I sit up in the darkness and I begin sketching—blindly pressing pencil to paper. I visualize images and then I sketch them. Only when the light of day allows a glimpse do I discover what I had created. These images, my morning discoveries, became a peaceful escape."

It was education that brought her and Mr. Hamdan to the United States. It was people believing in them along the way, as well as providing scholarships and loans to complement their mindset and drive what really helped them build a successful company. When they sold their company, they "decided to found Education Unbound because we believe education is the only wing that can make you fly. It can help you and help your family, no matter where you are. It can lift everybody around you, break the cycle of poverty and disadvantage." Its original mission was to "help increase the supply of high-tech talent through STEAM in education."

Mrs. Hamdan always dreamed of creating a more peaceful world in which we collaborate, empathize, and uplift. Just as the process of painting gave her an escape during her childhood, in 2016, she decided to also donate her art to Education Unbound, to help elevate a child out of the cycle of poverty and exploitation. She encourages us all to pay that feeling forward for underprivileged children so that they, too, can write their story, complete with joy and boundless opportunities.

The story gets more interesting and picks up steam, no pun intended, when the paths of the Hamdans cross with Ben Koch and Justin Vawter. Mr. Koch and Mr. Vawter founded

NuMinds in 2013 to start a revolution of awakening education through real, inspired learning. They were driven by the vision that NuMinds could provide a layer of enrichment beyond the school day, where real, inspired learning creates the conditions for life-long curiosity and self-development for both teachers and students. Mrs. Hamdan tells me that she was fortunate to find "two brilliant educators with the right heart and mind, plus the same mission and high energy levels."

I interviewed Mr. Koch, who is an admirer of Sir Ken Robinson (whose ideas on alternative education programs you may recall from other chapters in this book). So I understand as Mr. Koch energetically recounts how "the original business plan for NuMinds came to me and Justin in a flash of inspiration while on the way to the Rocky Racoon's one-hundred-mile race outside of Houston, Texas. We built it based on the EDvolution that we were aiming for. We were not seeking to replace the broken education system that we had experienced as educators, but to create a new system to complement it. One whose main purpose was to develop passionate and inspired innovators, not to standardize hearts and minds. We knew that STEAM was the best existing model to do this, and so we laid out a vision to transform by example, creating STEAM-based programs inspired by Sir Ken's concept of The Element."

After NuMinds and Education Unbound reached an agreement to collaborate in 2017, the passion was multiplied and the load of working as pioneers was distributed. This helped weather the storm of trials and tribulations natural to entrepreneurship. The fact that Mrs. Hamdan was an artist home-schooling her daughters after their Montessori school closed also helped fine-tune her understanding of STEM education as well as the business model transformation required. She recounts the story of visiting a well-respected independent school district and pitching how STEAM education could be used in their summer camps. None of the teachers or the administrators were familiar with the concept. Mr. Koch shared how "after that first summer of camps, where we inspired and excited children with STEAM, the parents would ask us, 'Why doesn't my kid like school this much?'"

Multiple proprietary programs have been developed based on the foundation of the "why" described above. The "how" is equally relevant. Mr. Koch explains it to me, drawing the simple yet powerful concepts on the white wall board at his office. The foundational element to inspire the kids and young adults alike is the individual that must meet three key criteria, which he draws as circles: passion, knowledge, and talent (or PKT). He leaves the intersection of the circles blank and smiles as he writes down the word Inspirators in the narrow PKT space, making it abundantly clear that he's not using the word teacher on purpose and notes that smiling is one of NuMind's core values.

The training for the inspirators is very well-defined and has been refined through sessions conducted across cultures in the United States, Argentina, and Lebanon. It consists of three pillars: STEAM, growth mindset, and creativity. It is worth explaining the basic idea of a growth mindset as elegantly described by Carol Dweck in her "Developing a Growth Mindset" talk.[73] A growth mindset in students means they are open

---

73   *Stanford Alumni*, "Developing a Growth Mindset with Carol Dweck," October 9, 2014, video, 9:37.

to processing errors, learning from them, and correcting the course as opposed to a fixed mindset, which is focused on test results and tends to run away from difficulties.

The result thus far is impressive, and the sky is the limit:

- 18,193 students and adults have been serviced through virtual programs, workshops, and camps.
- Five thousand educators have been invigorated, informed, and inspired in workshops, training sessions, and conferences.
- Eighty-three schools and community partners are part of the ecosystem.

I attended the first Mexican National STEAM Summit that took place in June 2020. It was a virtual event organized by Movimiento STEAM.

A Keynote, "Where is Mexico in STEAM Education," was delivered by Roberto Martínez Yllescas, Director of the Center of the Organization for Economic Cooperation and Development (OECD) in Mexico for Latin America.[74] He made it clear that Mexico must improve both its quantity and quality of STEM graduates to compete on a global stage. He also indicated that creativity is now recognized as a key skill for Mexico to rise and meet the challenges it's facing as a society. A staple skill in the artistic field, however a departure from past requirements for science and technology fields, where it wasn't given the same status as other cognitive skills.

---

74 Movimiento STEAM, "En dónde está México en Educación STEAM," June 18, 2020, video, 1:00:00.

I subsequently spoke with the founder Graciela Rojas Monte-
mayor in August 2020. The history of Mrs. Rojas and STEM
goes back to her childhood. Her father and three brothers
studied and practice in areas related to STEM. Graciela
seemed almost destined to study a career in those fields, but
she didn't feel identified with them. They were careers for
men. Despite having good performance and excellent grades,
she chose to study business administration.

At the age of nineteen, she graduated and started working.
At twenty-seven, she had reached a Director level position
at Terra Communications, and a short three years later, she
became Managing Director at a marketing agency. However,
one piece was missing, and she constantly wondered if she
was in the right place. She pondered whether she wanted to
dedicate herself to that career all her life to achieve a good
financial reward and recognition or pursue her true passion
for what she felt her soul had come to the world.

A personal crisis made her recall that as a child she wanted
to be a teacher. By destiny or coincidence, she met one of
Italy's first female physicians and a great world leader who
launched a whole pedagogical trend based on scientific
thought: Maria Montessori.

Mrs. Rojas became a Montessori teacher and a new adventure
began: To merge what she had studied with what she had
learned throughout her career. And that's how the Profesor
Chiflado enterprise was born (the English translation is the
Nutty Professor). It's an enterprise dedicated to making children's events where science is mixed into play—a dream that

encompassed marketing, her vocation for teaching, and the life project that made the most sense for her.

The road wasn't an easy one, yet Profesor Chiflado brought her great satisfaction: In 2014, Mrs. Rojas was awarded the National Entrepreneur Award and in 2015, the National Quality Award. In spite of the positive impact on millions of children, she still had an inkling to expand the category to impact people of different ages— a dream of going further and influencing public policy because she's a firm believer that STEAM is the way to achieve sustainable development and social well-being.

In 2017, Movimiento STEAM was born—a nonprofit association that seeks to promote STEAM education, the jobs of the future, and innovation through a vision of social impact and inclusion. This initiative led by Mrs. Rojas as President and Founder is a benchmark for STEAM education throughout Mexico and Latin America. One of its lines of action is to strategically link the multiple actors of society: National and international organizations, enterprises, research centers, and media among others, with the end goal to influence public policy and consolidate a regional strategy that promotes its vision.

That is how Movimiento STEAM has been integrating the STEAM ecosystem, and now more than 120 organizations, enterprises, and institutions work in a coordinated way to develop projects and actions to generate the exponential growth of STEAM education in Mexico.

In 2020, in alliance with the Varkey Foundation and the Global Edtech Impact Alliance, Movimiento STEAM launched the Extraordinary Teachers Award: National Teacher Prize Mexico with a lofty goal to illuminate the exceptional work of the teachers of Mexico in their classrooms. The Global Teacher Prize from the Varkey Foundation has become the Nobel Prize for education, and Movimiento STEAM is convinced that STEM areas are the ones with the greatest lag in our country and aware of the impact that teaching has on preventing school dropouts. Despite the COVID-19 pandemic, almost three thousand teacher nominations were received, and the award is supported by the Federal Ministry of Education as well as state education ministries.

Movimiento STEAM will continue to seek to recognize the exceptional work of women in these fields and on creating certifications, accreditations, and standards to ensure the quality of this education in Mexico and Latin America. Mrs. Rojas will continue to work tirelessly in favor of STEAM education, innovation, and the jobs of the future with a vision of social impact and inclusion. It is through the development of these competencies that labor inclusion can be attained, and with it, development for new generations with a special commitment to women.

Mrs. Rojas often shares, "STEAM is the solution to the problems that we live today, and although there is a long way to go, I know that together we will achieve STEAM for everyone, leaving no one behind. If I knew that there was something else that could change the planet more than STEAM education, I would dedicate myself to it. Since there isn't, I'm fully committed to it."

Movimiento STEAM has impacted more than twenty million people throughout Mexico and the region, and this is just the beginning of this great dream.

The STEAM movement is gaining speed, and the true intersection of art with technology is unleashing awesome possibilities to acquire twenty-first-century skills and abilities. I'm excited to be part of it, and I encourage you to join us!

Questions for Discussion

What challenges can we foresee in the near future if we don't encourage the intersection of arts and technology today?

What could happen in the near future if technology developers are not sensitive to the arts?

How should institutions reframe their approach to new technologies considering the importance that arts play?

What has been the impact on people, spaces, and places of operational programs that intersect art and technology?

Can arts serve as a connector among technologies?

How can arts be used to increase digital literacy?

How can arts be used to alleviate the unintended consequences of advanced technologies?

Can arts improve the human perception of virtual reality or augmented reality?

9

PURPOSE AND FAITH

———

Please take a moment to pray.

Did you pray from a place of faith or fear or anxiety? This is an important question because, in my experience, God doesn't respond to fear or anxiety. Is that your experience as well?

Do you know what happens when you combine the words "God" and "coincidence?" You have a "Diosidencia." Some call it "synchronicity" or events that appear to be connected yet have no causal connection.

"Diosidencia" is a very powerful word for me because I've experienced it on countless occasions. God loves us unconditionally and is working on our behalf whether we realize it or not. Sometimes it causes something good to happen, other times stopping something bad from happening. It respects our free will yet often laughs at our plans, particularly if they're not aligned with His purpose for us or His mission. Sometimes it allows us to experience pain, which transforms into purpose.

I am Catholic and want to share with you a tweet from Pope Francis:

"Faith is either missionary or it is no faith at all. Faith takes us out of ourselves and toward others. Faith must be transmitted, not to convince but to offer a treasure. Let us ask the Lord to help us live our faith with open doors: a transparent faith."[75]

POPE FRANCIS

If you're a Christian, you'll relate to the tweet from Pope Francis. If you're not, let me share a quote from a fellow Mexican American, born in Autlán, Jalisco, who I admire because of his mastery playing the guitar, as well as his search for self-discovery and enlightenment. In his autobiography *The Universal Tone*, he writes, "Love is the light that is inside of all of us, everyone. I salute the light that you are and that is inside your heart."[76]

---

75 Pope Francis (@Pontifex), "Faith is either missionary or it is no faith at all. Faith takes us out of ourselves and toward others. Faith must be transmitted, not to convince but to offer a treasure. Let us ask the Lord to help us live our faith with open doors: a transparent faith," Twitter, July 9, 2020.

76 Ashley Kahn, Carlos Santana, Hal Miller, *The Universal Tone: Bringing My Story to Light* (Orion Publishing Group, 2014).

This book captures stories of many individuals whose paths God has crossed with mine. For that, I'm very grateful. And you'll be able to read my story as well, but before you do, here's one more story that I find inspiring:

Debbie Renteria has always been a good student and known the importance of education; however, she couldn't follow a "traditional" path because she had to put her studies on hold to support her mom and younger brothers, to whom she's been like a second mom. She's even worked multiple jobs after they parted ways with her father. She hasn't always known what she wants, yet she's always been clear on what she doesn't want: Financial struggles or a job that she didn't like, for example. Both are equally important. Her mission is to hear people's stories because we all have one. She recalls reading in Chris Colfer's *The Land of Stories* series: "A villain is a victim whose story hasn't been told." This is a concept that she fully agrees with because there's always a villain in every story, and we don't know the heart and the foundation of what made them a villain.

Mrs. Renteria has a profound and peaceful demeanor, and it's not surprising, given that while recounting her story of following a non-traditional path, she told me that someone is always going to help you when in need. She says, "God is very good about putting the right people in your life at the right time, to either reignite your openness to hear encouraging words or to remind you to believe in yourself. It's almost human nature to sometimes doubt ourselves or think we're not worthy. And I heard that a lot. I heard I wasn't good enough. And you start to believe they may be right. I'm not that smart. I'm not this or that. I had to practice believing in myself. It really took practice and a lot of work. Right when I was just ready to quit, God was very good about strategically putting people in my life that reminded me I was good enough. It took a while, but I caught on and realized that I needed to say those words. We all need to speak them and say, 'Yes, I am.'" She calls it the law of attraction; if you want something, you have to say it and it'll come to you.

I asked Mrs. Renteria whether she had a role model or mentor, and she mentioned multiple names: Her mom; Mr. Castañon, who is the father of one of her best friends; Sister Patricia, who was the principal at her school; and Linda Bononcini, who was her mentor when she started teaching and continued to fill that role until she retired. A common message that she received from her mom and from Sister Patricia was, "You're destined for greatness." Mr. Castañon used to tell her how smart she was. Linda always made a point to lend Mrs. Renteria a hand whenever she seemed to need it and proved a great example of a teacher and administrator. She found ways to always be creative and never lose sight of the best outcome for the students.

There is no doubt that Mrs. Renteria is a special human being. Is she more special than you or could it be that you only have not paid enough attention like she did to folks who have tried to encourage you along the way? Or do you just need to practice it more? After all, she clearly stated that to achieve it, "I had to practice believing in myself. It really took practice and a lot of work."

Being a man of faith myself, I jumped at the opportunity to learn how she developed her faith. Very quickly and confidently,

Mrs. Renteria replied: "My mother was the one who instilled it in us, and I did go to a small little Catholic school." Her grandmother was a big part of Mrs. Renteria's life and was the one who insisted she go to a Catholic school despite it being a stretch financially. Mrs. Renteria shares how one day she was called to the principal's office over the public announcement system. Her friends were surprised and immediately thought that Mrs. Renteria was in trouble. Mrs. Renteria didn't recall having done anything wrong, however got very nervous and her heart was pounding as she walked to meet with Sister Patricia who, despite being a petite person, instilled fear in all students. Once she arrived in Sister Patricia's office, Sister Patricia proceeded to tell Mrs. Renteria that her dad was again late with her tuition payment and that her balance had reached a new high. Mrs. Renteria felt ashamed and powerless. She had been doing work at the school already to help pay off her education, cleaning the kitchen and the restrooms. She humbly apologized, with her head bowed in shame.

She thought she would be expelled; however, she couldn't believe what she heard. Mrs. Renteria chokes a bit as she recounts that Sister Patricia told her she really wanted Mrs. Renteria to continue studying at the school and she would eliminate her debt on two conditions: One that she continue being the great student she was and, two, that no one else found out about it. Sister Patricia went on to say that if anyone ever asked her about it, she would deny it, and in addition, Mrs. Renteria said, now chuckling, it would be her responsibility for making a nun lie.

To close the interview, Mrs. Renteria asked me to share this thought with you: "We're definitely here for a purpose. The hard part is finding the answer to 'What is my purpose? Or 'Why am I here?' I would invite anyone that feels she or he doesn't have a purpose to open up and connect with themselves and with others. You will find the right people out there that will be there to help you! Have faith when you ask for it. Say 'Lord guide me, direct me to what I'm supposed to do. I want to be your faithful servant in whatever way you created me to do. Show me what that is.' It might change. For a season, it might be here and for another, it might be there, but you'll find it. Once you find it, just never give up."

I couldn't agree more with Mrs. Renteria because I'm the farthest away from a self-made man as you can possibly find. I've always found the right people, and it's a blessing to connect the dots looking back.

I grew up Catholic in Mexico. I have both of my grandmothers, my abuelas "Nena" and "Mamita," as we called them, to thank for the faith component of my upbringing. I wandered away from my faith until one fine day when too many dark clouds had formed over my head and Jesus decided to take firm action. It was 2006 when I had an accident, hit my head, and found myself asking three questions over and over as my wife recounts. To this day, I have a memory gap that spans hours before and after the accident. My family and I had come back to Dallas in 2004 after assignments with Ericsson in France, Mexico, and Guatemala. I was really struggling financially as an entrepreneur, and it was starting to show in my marriage. The fortunate consequences of the accident were that the dark clouds disappeared, and I came back to my faith. Jesus reset me. I recall vividly giving thanks for the blessing at our parish of Saint Joseph Catholic in Garland.

Within a matter of weeks after the accident, I received *The Purpose Driven Life* by Rick Warren as a gift.[77] I read it and started wondering what my purpose was. I registered for a Bible class at Bible Study Fellowship International (BSF) and chose it because I wanted to have a non-denominational point of view of the Bible's teachings. In 2007, we moved to Indianapolis where I took a job with ACS (now Xerox). I continued with my BSF course and searching for my purpose as I continued my executive career.

Fast forward to 2015 and my heart journey accelerated thanks to a chi-kung crash course with Sifu Rama on which I participated as part of an executive retreat. Chi means energy, and chi-kung is a technique that involves movement exercises, breathing, and meditation. It took place at the Blue Mountain in Costa Rica, which is the place that Sifu Rama chose, among other things, due to the positive energy flow that exists in that peaceful place on earth. I recall having abdominal cramps, which I had never experienced before. Sifu Rama told me, "Good. You're opening up energy flows that were blocked."

In 2017, I was gifted the book *Halftime* by Bob Buford.[78] I took it with me on a year-end family vacation to Tequila, Mexico. No, I wasn't drunk while reading it in case you're wondering. The world-famous tequila beverage has an appellation of origin and comes from the town of Tequila in the state of Jalisco.

---

77   Rick Warren, *The Purpose Driven Life* (Zondervan, 2002).
78   Bob Buford, *Halftime* (Zondervan, 2015).

I loved the book *Halftime* for multiple reasons. It really struck a nerve on more than one occasion as I flipped page after page. I could have read the book like a novel you can't put down in a matter of hours. However, I was no longer using only my head. I was definitely feeling a strong pull from my heart. I often had to pause and reflect on the many concepts and stories. It was inspirational, and having recently invested in an AI company, my mind wandered in multiple directions. I was being present with my family since we were having a really fun time, yet looking back at the past and praying for guidance about the future.

Another reason I loved *Halftime* is that I read Bob Buford, the author, had been a disciple of Peter Drucker. I admire Mr. Drucker for the many reasons I mentioned in the first chapter, and my favorite book happens to be his *Adventures of a Bystander*. Morton Meyerson recommended it to a group of Monterrey Tec alumni (ExATecs DFW) while giving us a chat at the Meyerson Symphony Center in Dallas, Texas in 2005.

I was pleasantly surprised to find out that Bob Buford founded the Halftime Institute in Irving, Texas, where they have multiple programs to help "halftimers" go from success to significance, following a methodology based on the concepts that Mr. Buford captured in his book. When we came back home to Dallas after our year-end vacation, I started researching the institute. It looked very cool, particularly their twelve-month "fellows" flagship program.

Time flies when you're having fun, and when in mid-2018 my then-CEO Andres Ruzo asked whether I would want to take an advancement certificate at an institution focused on conscious capitalism, I asked whether he would allow a substitution. I explained that I would derive the same benefit from the Halftime fellows program, which was very similar to the one he proposed, with two added benefits: It was faith-based and included some sessions for my wife. Mr. Ruzo liked the idea given his strong sense of both faith and family.

In October 2018, I started the fellows program at the Halftime Institute. I couldn't give enough thanks to the Lord. It came at a very difficult time for me at home, given challenges that my wife and I, as empty nesters, were facing with both our sons. I was getting so much energy from the program—energy that I needed to deal with those challenges. I must have bored more than one person while describing the program to friends and family, yet not many understood it.

In early 2019, my mission was becoming clearer, and by mid-March, it was crystal clear: Following the great commandment and increasing economic growth and social inclusion for young adults in disadvantaged areas of the US and Mexico. At the same time, there were changes happening at work, which led to a flurry of thoughts and feelings. I prayed constantly for guidance and was in constant communication with my Halftime brothers, my coach Rod Stewart, and the "personal board" that I had assembled. Surrendering, I learned, is a necessary step toward significance. I had clarity on my mission yet no certainty. Being at that point and not taking a leap of faith could be interpreted as disobedience. The carrot and the stick. On Good Friday, I resigned to embark on the full-time pursuit of my mission.

There are multiple ways to find your purpose. In my case, it's been a mix of faith and pain. Regardless of what path you follow, have faith and you will find your purpose! May God bless you.

Questions for Discussion

What were you passionate about as a child?

Think about a painful experience that you've gone through. Are the lessons learned valuable to help other individuals?

If you knew that you had only one more year of life, would you want to continue doing what you are presently doing?

What do your closest relationships tell you about what you excel at?

APPENDIX 1 – THE KOSMOS WAY

Kosmos is a social venture cofounded with my partners, Adriana de Urquidi aka Adri, and Nicolas Gonzalez aka Nic. It's the intersection of art, technology, and opportunity—an opportunity for disengaged young adults in disadvantaged areas of the United States and Mexico.

The definition of opportunity is "a set of circumstances that make it possible to do something." In order to do anything, first and foremost, you must want to do it. Needing to do something isn't enough. You must want it. That is how our free will works, and even more so for disengaged Gen Zs whose circumstances keep changing and on top of it are being impacted by the slingshot effect.

I met Nic in June 2019 when he gave a talk about his experience as a young Hispanic artist at Mercado 369 in the Oak Cliff neighborhood of Dallas. Nic's story in Chapter 4, "Art and Education" should give you a good understanding of why his artistic background and upbringing complement my technology background and upbringing shared in the Introduction and in Chapter 9, "Purpose and Faith."

I met Adri at a Hispanic Leadership Summit at Southern Methodist University (SMU) in September of that same year. Adri not only brings the much-needed gender diversity to the team, but more importantly, a wealth of experience in social programs, systems analysis, and contacts developed while she was a global shaper at the World Economic Forum.

Adri, Nic, and I agreed to become partners in September 2019.

What makes Kosmos unique is its methodology to braid the arts with technology. The vehicle is a twelve-month technology apprenticeship that develops a skill that allows young adults to reengage and join the labor market doing remote work. This work and training are completed without them leaving their communities, which is of utmost importance to prevent brain drain. But more importantly, by braiding carefully designed artistic exercises along the twelve months, the young adults develop twenty-first-century skills that will help them for life: curiosity, collaboration and communication, and critical and creative thinking.

Kosmos partners with arts centers already established in their communities and working with young adults who are artistically inclined. They find disengaged young adults in their community who have tried the arts program and failed or have knocked on their door to inquire whether they have a technology program. All young adults nowadays have technology skills by mere virtue of their interaction with technology, whether it's screens, gaming consoles, or internet of things (IoT) devices. We jointly apply an assessment to determine the match for the Kosmos program and select the "techies" who can benefit from it.

A common question we are asked is how the artists are making time to learn tech skills. They don't have to. Kosmos doesn't train the artists in the art centers. It trains the young adults who don't want to be artists, or who have tried the arts program only to determine that it's not for them.

The artist entrepreneur described in Chapter 2, "Art and Culture Improving Communities" is a cornerstone of the program. He or she has done the real heavy lifting of getting established in a community and knowing its valuable assets, of which human capital is the most important. And above all, gaining the trust of the community. These experienced artists provide a positive space under which the techies reside at least once a week. Artists and techies are under the same roof, effectively bringing down any natural barriers that exist between them and allowing their minds to be open to collaboration. The rural pilot program that successfully culminated in the mountains of Guerrero, Mexico in June 2020 proved there is a virtuous circle in having artists and techies under the same roof.

The rubric followed for the development of twenty-first-century skills covers the three aforementioned pillars, and their progress from basic to intermediate to advanced in each of them. While the confidence critical for a success mindset isn't spelled out in the rubric, the young adults gain it while advancing on their tech skills and pillars.

The method to braid arts and technology has been refined after a lengthy systems analysis, countless hours of development, and verification with subject-matter experts. It considers all the elements of successful alternative programs described by Sir Ken Robinson covered in Chapter 4, "Art and Education":

- Personalization
- Strong support for the teachers
- Close links with the community
- Broad and diverse curriculum
- Often programs that involve students outside of school as well as inside

The next step for the venture is to validate the method through an urban pilot in South Dallas. In addition to the standard entrepreneurial tribulations, the COVID-19 pandemic has impacted Kosmos mainly in the form of delays. For example, we use office space out of the Incubator at SMU, located on the seventh floor of the East Campus Tower, across the highway from the main campus and the George W. Bush Presidential Library. We have a phenomenal coworking space with a great view of the "Hilltop" north of downtown Dallas where the university was built. The incubator was closed for months, making it difficult to have much-needed collaboration meetings for which technology is no substitute.

Even if the coworking space had been open, we all had personal challenges that needed attention. For example, we jokingly ask Adri whether she only has two kids, because when she joined phone calls or web meetings from home, it sounded as if she had ten kids in her surroundings.

It is of extreme importance to validate the Kosmos model before scaling. First and foremost because the most important thing any young adult going through an alternative program deserves is to be put in a position to succeed. After two failed attempts at securing an artist entrepreneur in South Dallas capable and excited to be part of the pilot, we located the ideal partner. The third time's the charm. We expect the urban pilot to begin the moment this book is published. Is it another "Diosidencia" as described in Chapter 9, "Purpose and Faith"?

Four years after Nic's graduation from SMU with a bachelor's in fine arts, and two decades after my graduation from the same alma mater with a master's in business administration, we conducted the interview that allowed me to reflect Nic's story in this book. Nic was overlooking the campus with a big smile on his face. We were in the same building he used to clean as part of his janitorial duties twenty years ago.

There are some dots we can connect looking back. We cannot connect dots looking forward. However, if passion is a leading indicator of success, the Kosmos team has it in abundance. We're encouraged by the bonds we've formed as a team, the results thus far, and the encouraging feedback we continue receiving.

APPENDIX 2 – CITATIONS

Introduction

Caplan, Bryan. "The World Might Be Better Off Without College for Everyone." *The Atlantic,* January/February 2018. https://www.theatlantic.com/magazine/archive/2018/01/whats-college-good-for/546590/.

CollegeAtlas. "U.S. College Dropout Rate and Dropout Statistics." Updated Jun 29th, 2018. Accessed September 10, 2020. https://www.collegeatlas.org/college-dropout.html.

DoSomething. "11 Facts about High School Dropout Rates." Accessed September 10, 2020. https://www.dosomething.org/us/facts/11-facts-about-high-school-dropout-rates.

OECD. "Higher Education in Mexico: Labour Market Relevance and Outcomes." Accessed October 15, 2020. https://www.oecd.org/fr/publications/higher-education-in-mexico-9789264309432-en.htm.

TED. "How a Handful of Tech Companies Control Billions of Minds Every Day | Tristan Harris." Jul 28, 2017. Video, 17:00. https://youtu.be/C74amJRp730.

Chapter 1

Apple Inc. "Apple Presents iPod." Accessed October 15, 2020. https://www.apple.com/newsroom/2001/10/23Apple-Presents-iPod/.

BBC. "Netflix's History: From DVD Rentals to Streaming Success." January 23, 2018. Accessed October 15, 2020. http://www.bbc.co.uk/newsbeat/article/42787047/netflixs-history-from-dvd-rentals-to-streaming-success.

Bezos, Jeff. "Person of the Year." *Time,* December 27, 1999. https://time.com/vault/year/1999/.

Brinkley, Joel. "U.S. vs. Microsoft: The Overview; U.S. Judge Says Microsoft Violated Antitrust Laws with Predatory Behavior." *The New York Times.* April 4, 2000. https://www.nytimes.com/2000/04/04/business/us-vs-microsoft-overview-us-judge-says-microsoft-violated-antitrust-laws-with.html.

Buford, Bob. *Stuck in Halftime: Reinventing Your One and Only Life.* Grand Rapids, Michigan: Zondervan Publishing House, 2001.

CNN. "Google's Incredible Growth: A Timeline." Accessed October 15, 2020. https://www.cnn.com/interactive/2018/12/business/google-history-timeline/index.html.

Encyclopedia Britannica Online. PlayStation2 Electronic Gaming Console. Accessed October 15, 2020.https://www. britannica.com/topic/PlayStation-2.

Forbes Mexico. "El 75% de adolescentes y padres mexicanos, adictos al celular." Accessed October 15, 2020. https://www.forbes.com.mx/ el-75-de-adolescentes-y-padres-mexicanos-adictos-al-celular/.

Kushleva, Kostadin, Hunter, John F., Proulx, Jason, Pressman, Sarah D., Dunn, Elizabeth. "Smartphones Reduce Smiles Between Strangers." Elsevier, Computers in Human Behavior, Volume 91, February 2019. https://www.sciencedirect.com/ science/article/abs/pii/S0747563218304643.

Pew Research. "Artificial Intelligence and the Future of Humans." Accessed October 15, 2020. https://www.pewresearch.org/internet/2018/12/10/ artificial-intelligence-and-the-future-of-humans/.

Pew Research. "Teens, Social Media & Technology 2018." Accessed October 15, 2020. https://www.pewresearch. org/internet/2018/05/31/teens-social-media-technology-2018/.

Chapter 2

Chatterton, Tim; Newmarch, Georgia. "The Future Is Already Here – It's Just Not Very Evenly Distributed." ACM Interactions, March/April 2017. https://interactions.acm.org/archive/view/march-april-2017/the-future-is-already-here.

Cullinan, Deborah. "CultureBank: A Vision for a New Investment System." Federal Reserve Bank of San Francisco Community Development Innovation Review 2019-2. https://doi.org/10.24148/cdir2019-02.

HowlRound Theatre Commons. "Arts Culture & Community Investment – Culturebank Dallas with IgniteArts Dallas." February 25, 2020. Video, 2:56. https://youtu.be/4uJ2rW2sp3Y.

Rosendo, Bernardo. *Esperanza en la Montaña. Rescate Cultural y Formación para el Trabajo.* Mexico: Luna Media Comunicación, 2018.

Tornatore Giuseppe, dir. *Cinema Paradiso.* Les Films Ariane, 1988.

Chapter 3

Boyle Danny, dir. *Steve Jobs.* Universal Pictures. 2015.

Chromoscopic adapter for television equipment patent US2296019A filed by Guillermo Gonzalez Camarena on August 14, 1941.

History.com. "These Women Taught Depression-Era Americans to Use Electricity." Accessed October 15, 2020. https://www.history.com/news/new-deal-great-depression-rural-electrification.

International Youth Foundation. "2016 Global Millennial Viewpoints Survey." Accessed October 15, 2020. https://www.iyfnet.org/library/2016-global-millennial-viewpoints-survey.

Kubrick, Stanley, dir. *2001: A Space Odyssey.* Metro-Goldwyn-Mayer. 1968.

Sheldon, Pavica, Honeycutt, James M. *The Dark Side of Social Media* San Diego: Elsevier, 2019.

TED. "How a Handful of Tech Companies Control Billions of Minds Every Day | Tristan Harris." Jul 28, 2017. Video, 17:00. https://youtu.be/C74amJRp730.

TVEAPFilms. "The Last Public Message Recorded by Sir Arthur C Clarke" circa 2009. Video, 9:01. https://www.youtube.com/watch?v=0F2z5-kTm2I.

Twenge, Jean M. "Have Smartphones Destroyed a Generation?" *The Atlantic,* September 2017. https://www.theatlantic.com/magazine/archive/2017/09/has-the-smartphone-destroyed-a-generation/534198/.

YOU, "Person of the Year." *Time,* December 25, 2006. https://time.com/vault/year/2006/.

Chapter 4

Camnitzer, Luis. *Visiting Minds 2013. Radical Pedagogy.* Panama: Sarigua, 2013.

Emler, Trina E., Yong Zhao, Jiayi Deng, Danqing Yin, and Yurou Wang. "Side Effects of Large-Scale Assessments in Education." *ECNU Review of Education* 2, no. 3, September 2019. https://doi.org/10.1177/2096531119878964.

Sackner, Sara dir. *Jay W. Jensen and the future of arts education in America.* Sackner Films Inc. 2007.

TED. "How to Escape Education's Death Valley | Sir Ken Robinson." May 10, 2013. Video. 19:11. https://youtu.be/wX78iKhInsc.

Chapter 5

Canal22. "Documental 1968-1971. Los Jefes del Rock." May 14, 2009. Video. 49:3. https://www.youtube.com/watch?v=7-u5MQx1J14.

Carpenter, Christopher J., and Chandra S. Amaravadi. "A Big Data Approach to Assessing the Impact of Social Norms: Reporting One's Exercise to a Social Media Audience." *Communication Research* 46, no. 2, March 2019. https://doi.org/10.1177/0093650216657776.

Durman, Tyler. *Counterintuitive. What 4 Million Teenagers Wish We Knew: Bite-Sized Wisdom 4 Parents and Teachers.* Laguna Beach, California: BSWisdom Books, 2015.

TED. "The Mysterious Workings of the Adolescent Brain – Sarah-Jayne Blakemore." June 1, 2013. Video. 14:26. https://youtu.be/6oKsikHollM.

Chapter 6

De Chateaubriand, Francois. *Memories Beyond the Grave.* 1849-1850.

The success quote attributed to Ralph Waldo Emerson could have been an original quote from Bessie Anderson Stanley.

Chapter 7

Caplan, Bryan. "The World Might Be Better Off Without College for Everyone." *The Atlantic,* January/February 2018. https://www.theatlantic.com/magazine/archive/2018/01/whats-college-good-for/546590/.

CollegeAtlas. "U.S. College Dropout Rate and Dropout Statistics." Updated Jun 29, 2018. Accessed September 10, 2020. https://www.collegeatlas.org/college-dropout.html.

Crockett, Ana, Ryder Perlmeter, Emily, Hubbert Doyle, Molly. "Opportunity Youth in Texas." *Federal Reserve Bank of Dallas.* October 2019.

DoSomething. "11 Facts About High School Dropout Rates." Accessed September 10, 2020. https://www.dosomething.org/us/facts/11-facts-about-high-school-dropout-rates.

Harari, Yuval Noah. *21 Lessons for the 21st Century*. New York: Penguin Random House, 2018.

"How to Adopt Skills-based Hiring Practices." Society for Human Resource Management. Accessed October 15, 2020. https://www.shrm.org/hr-today/news/hr-magazine/0318/pages/hiring-for-skills-not-pedigree.aspx.

https://www.garlandisdschools.net/grctc.

https://generalassemb.ly/.
https://www.kenzie.academy/.
https://flatironschool.com/.
https://www.holbertonschool.com/.
https://www.hackreactor.com/.

https://techgenies.com/techbridge-coding.

https://www.cloudfactory.com/.
https://www.samasource.com/.

https://nxtlevelsa.org/.
https://restoreeducation.org/.
https://jovenesconstruyendoelfuturo.stps.gob.mx/.

Instituto de Educación de Aguascalientes, Webinar ¿ Quo Vadis - Educatio? - Educación Dual y Formación Profesional Continua – versus Formación clásica Universitaria, July 31, 2020, 1:02:00. https://m.facebook.com/story.php?story_fbid=900877437064949&id=117452238331915&refid=12&_tn_=%2As%2As.

Niranjan, Ajit. "What Is Germany's Dual Education System — and Why Do Other Countries Want It?" *Deutsche Welle,* April 6, 2018. https://www.dw.com/en/what-is-germanys-dual-education-system-and-why-do-other-countries-want-it/a-42902504.

OECD. "Higher Education in Mexico: Labour Market Relevance and Outcomes." Accessed October 15, 2020. https://www.oecd.org/fr/publications/higher-education-in-mexico-9789264309432-en.htm.

"Opportunity Pathways Background Paper." Strada Education Network. Accessed October 15, 2020. https://www.opportunitypathways.org/.

RSA (Royal Society for the encouragement of Arts, Manufactures and Commerce). "Ian Leslie on Why We Must Continue to Learn and Be Curious." June 18, 2014. Video. 19:7. https://www.youtube.com/watch?v=1JT_4owlxYY.

Spees, Ann-Cathrin. "Could Germany's Vocational Education and Training System Be a Model for the U.S.?" *World Education News + Reviews,* June 12, 2018. https://wenr.wes.org/2018/06/could-germanys-vocational-education-and-training-system-be-a-model-for-the-u-s.

Tencer, Daniel. "85% of Jobs That Will Exist in 2030 Haven't Been Invented Yet: Dell." *Huffington Post.* July 14th, 2017. https://www.huffingtonpost.ca/2017/07/14/85-of-jobs-that-will-exist-in-2030-haven-t-been-invented-yet-d_a_23030098/.

Chapter 8

Eger, John M. "National Science Foundation Slowly Turning STEM to STEAM." *The Huffington Post,* May 31, 2011. https://www.huffpost.com/entry/national-science-foundati_b_868449.

Movimiento STEAM. "En dónde está México en Educación STEAM." June 18, 2020. Video. 1:00:00. https://youtu.be/dGuoxFSoJOs.

"Reinvesting in Arts Education: Winning America's Future Through Creative Schools." Obama Whitehouse Archives blog. Accessed October 15, 2020. https://obamawhitehouse.archives.gov/blog/2011/05/12/reinvesting-arts-education-winning-america-s-future-through-creative-schools.

Stanford Alumni. "Developing a Growth Mindset with Carol Dweck." October 9, 2014. Video. 9:37. https://youtu.be/hiiEeMN7vbQ.

Chapter 9

Buford, Bob. *Halftime.* Zondervan, 2015.

Kahn, Ashley, Santana, Carlos, Miller, Hal. *The Universal Tone: Bringing My Story to Light.* Orion Publishing Group: 2014.

Pope Francis (@Pontifex), "Faith is either missionary or it is no faith at all. Faith takes us out of ourselves and toward others. Faith must be transmitted, not to convince but to offer a treasure. Let us ask the Lord to help us live our faith with open doors: a transparent faith," Twitter, July 9, 2020.

Warren, Rick. *The Purpose Driven Life.* Zondervan, 2002.

CPSIA information can be obtained
at www.ICGtesting.com
Printed in the USA
LVHW021941190521
687896LV00013B/1716